For Any Young Mother
Who Lives in a Shoe

For Any Young Mother
Who Lives in a Shoe

A Christian Survival Guide

Mary Tobey Marsh

Judson Press ® Valley Forge

For Any Young Mother Who Lives in a Shoe
A Christian Survival Guide

Copyright © 1991
Judson Press, Valley Forge, PA 19482-0851

Bible quotations in this volume are from

Good News Bible, the Bible in Today's English Version. Copyright © American Bible Society 1966, 1971, 1976.

Revised Standard Version of the Bible, copyrighted 1946, 1952, © 1971, 1973 by the Division of Christian Education of the National Council of the Churches of Christ in the U.S.A., and used by permission.

HOLY BIBLE New International Version, copyright © 1978, New York International Bible Society. Used by permission.

The Holy Bible, King James Version.

Library of Congress Cataloging-in-Publication Data
Marsh, Mary Tobey, 1960–
  For any young mother who lives in a shoe : a Christian survival guide / by Mary Tobey Marsh.
    p.   cm.
  Includes bibliographical references.
  ISBN 0-8170-1170-6
  1. Mothers—Religious life.   2. Parenting—Religious aspects-
-Christianity.   3. Christian life—1960–   I. Title.
BV4529.M35   1991
248.8'431—dc20
                            91-10149
                              CIP

The name JUDSON PRESS is registered as a trademark in the U.S. Patent Office.
Printed in the U.S.A.

To Lewwy,

A number one husband and father.
This book would not have been possible without you,
in more ways than just three.

-»> Contents «<-

⤳≫ Preface ≪⤶

When I first began to write this book, I envisioned a book to make the preschool mother laugh. I saw my book as a humor book, to ease the reader's burden through laughter. As I wrote, however, and as I continued to live the life of a preschool mother, I was constantly reminded of how important and serious my job as mother really was. Besides that, after a full day of dealing with three preschoolers, I didn't always feel like laughing by the time I sat down at my computer.

I still feel that a sense of humor is essential to me in my parenting, in dealing with my children and in taking the difficulties in stride. But I recognize that I need much more than that: I need to remember how important my job is; I need spiritual, emotional, and intellectual support; I need encouragement; and most of all, I need to have God standing beside me every step of the way.

I hope that your job as a mother is made easier by laughter and encouragement in this book. I hope you'll remember that you're not alone in your task: God is with you, and other mothers are struggling, too. I hope you can recognize some of your own plight and joys in these pages and be uplifted by knowing, "Hey! Somebody else feels that way, too!"

So humor is merely the sugar in the cake batter for my book. My guidance from God is the flour, my ideas are the milk, my thoughts are the butter, my suggestions are the salt (too many of them may harden your arteries), my stories are the flavoring, and my writing is the baking powder. Your thoughts of your children as you read will become the icing. I've never made a real cake from scratch, but I couldn't find a Betty Crocker mix that would work for a book, so here is my **Shoe** from scratch.

I pray that this cake will "hit the spot" for you. ❧

⇢≫ Part I ≪⇠
There Was a Young Mother Who Lived in a Shoe: Encouragement!

There was a young mother who lived in a shoe.
She had too many children to know what to do.
She gave them Spaghetti-O's without any cheese,
She screamed bloody murder and turned on TV.

If you're a young mother who lives in a shoe,
Who feels like your household resembles a zoo,
Then hope lies within the words written here
That you're not alone in frustrations or fears.

You may have one child, or ten may be yours.
You may cope on your own or have help with your chores.
Whatever your spot, it may help you to see
That others relate—God, mothers, and me. ⇝

⇸≫ 1 ≪↞
On Being a Preschool Mother

. . . Of his own free will he gave up all he had,
  and took the nature of a servant.
He became like man
  and appeared in human likeness.
      —Philippians 2:7 (GNB)
      ⇸≫ ≪↞

Perhaps the title should be "On Being the Mother of Preschoolers." But I enjoy watching "Sesame Street"; I cheered at Maria and Luis's wedding and when they had their baby; I cried when the Little Mermaid married her prince; I'm more likely to blow the family budget on toys and kids' books than on my clothes, and my favorite movies are *Bambi* and *The Land Before Time.* I greet my husband at the door with "Where's the blue dinosaur?" or "Let's go out to eat tonight! Pleeeeeease?" I regularly use words like "poop" and "pee-pee" and "yucky" and "doggie." So perhaps I am a "preschool mother" after all. At the end of a day with three preschoolers my cerebrum must certainly resemble a ball of clay.

Yet, what if I didn't occasionally use words like "kitty" or "choo-choo"? What if I didn't sit on the floor and build roadways and train tracks? What if I didn't pretend to be Bambi's mother, or to drink coffee from a thimble-size cup, or to forget an answer to a question so I wouldn't win the game? If I never did any of these, how could I really communicate with my kids? How could I communicate to them the knowledge that they are important, that their activities and ideas count, that they are worth my time and energies?

So what if the size of the average word I speak has shrunk to three letters? As my children grow, so will the size of our vocabulary words. In fifteen years they will be beating me at Trivial Pursuit. And because I have spent time with them and have communicated to them how important and full of worth their God has made them, we will continue to communicate, to share, and to play, at ever-expanding and deepening levels. And when someday, one of them says, "Mom, I have a problem and I really need to talk to you," then I'll smile to myself and know that my time as a preschool mother was worth it after all. ई

➤➤➤ 2 ⫷⫷⫷
You're Not the Only One

*No temptation has overtaken you that is not common to man.
God is faithful, and he will not let you be tempted beyond your
strength, but with the temptation will also provide the way of
escape, that you may be able to endure it.*
— *1 Corinthians 10:13 (RSV)*

➤➤➤ ⫷⫷⫷

Misery loves company. Yes, and misery needs company. When
misery discovers that it is in very good company, it rejoices at the
load that seems, if not lighter, at least more bearable.

I don't feel quite right in calling preschool motherhood a time
of misery, yet it is a time of distinct and inevitable stresses. Imperfect children are given to imperfect women who often expect
themselves to be perfect mothers and their offspring to be perfect
children. In high school math I was taught that two negatives
multiplied together resulted in a positive. This is not supported by
the results of human reproduction. More appropriate is the math
principle that two negatives added to each other result in a third
negative.

Most of us are keenly aware of our own imperfect status and
how far we are from the ideal we strive for. We are each intimately
aware of our own faults, frustrated by our powerlessness over
them and by their omnipresence. If we were to sit down and
enumerate our flaws and mistakes, most of us would get quite
discouraged. We know the times when we lose patience with our
children, snap at our husbands, scream like crazy women. We
know how often we feel discouraged, count our trials instead of
our blessings, and wonder how on earth we'll ever survive.

God promises us: "My grace is sufficient for you, for my
power is made perfect in weakness" (2 Corinthians 12:9, NIV).
God can also help us to conquer our frailties. But because we
are human, and because God is by choice not a puppeteer, our
ultimate conquest of all our imperfections will not come in this
lifetime.

Yet this is hard to remember when we see other women that
seem to be pillars of faith and perfection. We may glance at

another woman and think, *She has it so together. How in the world does she do it? Why can't I be like that?*

What we often forget is that we see other people's best sides and our own worst sides. I know my own worst thoughts and the times when I fail—but very few others do. Others see my best side and may even think that I am one who has it all together. I put my best foot forward. So does everyone else.

A concrete example of this is housecleaning. When I know someone is coming over, I make the extra effort to straighten and clean the house. If my husband and I have a group of people over for a special occasion, they probably get the impression (unless they look too closely) of a basically tidy and well-kept house, and do not realize that this is not the norm for the Marsh residence. When I go to someone else's house, I will notice its tidiness, its cleanliness, and think, *Oh, why doesn't my house look neat like hers?* It doesn't fully occur to me that this may not be the norm for her residence either.

This "best-foot-forward syndrome" often robs us of our best salve—the realization that others are struggling like we are. As C.S. Lewis expresses it in *Surprised by Joy,* "Nothing, I suspect, is more astonishing in any man's life than the discovery that there do exist people very, very like himself."[1] Or as Lucy Maude Montgomery's Anne of Green Gables says, we long for a kindred spirit.[2]

I felt absolutely liberated when I learned how Abby Adams, daughter-in-law of John Quincy Adams, the sixth president of the United States, struggled in her duties as mother. Listen to her struggles and experience your own liberation.

Abby's tribulation began after the birth of her second child, and worsened after the third child.

The scampers of the children now were a bother to Charles Francis as well as to Abby. Once so eager for youngsters, the young parents decided to take a holiday from them. . . . After traveling two thousand miles, the vacationers grew weary as the trip closed, but Abby shrank from returning to her children. She begged Charles to give her some laudanum, the tincture of opium used at the time to relieve stress and pain. It would "carry her on," she implored, gratefully taking the twenty drops Charles doled out.[3]

[After her next child] Abby shrank from resuming a daily regimen dominated by four small children. . . . She held back from leaving her room, causing Charles to observe, "She seems rather disposed to magnify her own evils, and that almost without any exercise of will." Only after nearly a month had passed did Abby attempt to sit up in bed.[4]

Abby's physical and emotional health returned, but after the birth of number five, her "cheerfulness" left her as she faced the daily care of five young children.[5]

As I read of Abby's struggles, I felt relieved and even invigorated. *Someone else struggled too,* I thought. *I'm not alone! In fact, I seem to be doing well, relatively speaking!* I had found a fellow struggler.

I imagined sharing notes with Abby Adams about the struggles of motherhood. Yes, Abby had servants to help care for her charges, but she did not have diaper service, baby wipes, baby swings, or educational toys. Abby had a cook and a gardener, but she did not have fast food, a washing machine, a car, or a television.

In spite of the changes, the pressures, I'm sure, are changeless. "Mommy!" demand five children at once. "Momma, Sister touched me!" "Mommy, I wet my pants." "Waa! I don't like chicken! I want something else for dinner!" "Momma, where's my toy gun? Oh, here it is. Bang! Bang! You're dead."

Happily, Abby's motherhood experience did finally take a permanent turn for the better:

Eventually, aided by time, religious faith, and support from Louisa [her mother-in-law] and Charles, Abby not only regained her spirit but advanced to a new independence. . . . [Charles] was amazed by this seemingly new wife, whom he pronounced "better than I ever knew her."[6]

Yes, others struggle with motherhood, too. Yes, women do survive the preschool years. And yes, they come out better than ever. Our time is coming, too! &

⇢≫ 3 ≪←
Preschool Mother, You Are Not Alone

O LORD, you have searched me
  and you know me.
You know when I sit and when I rise;
  you perceive my thoughts from afar.
You discern my going out and my lying down;
  you are familiar with all my ways.
Before a word is on my tongue
  you know it completely, O LORD.

You hem me in, behind and before;
  you have laid your hand upon me.
Such knowledge is too wonderful for me,
  too lofty for me to attain.

Where can I go from your Spirit?
  Where can I flee from your presence?
If I go up to the heavens, you are there;
  if I make my bed in the depths, you are there.
If I rise on the wings of the dawn,
  if I settle on the far side of the sea,
Even there your hand will guide me,
  your right hand will hold me fast.

If I say, "Surely the darkness will hide me
  and the light become night around me,"
even the darkness will not be dark to you;
  the night will shine like the day,
  for darkness is as light to you.

For you created my inmost being;
  you knit me together in my mother's womb.
I praise you because I am fearfully and wonderfully made;
  your works are wonderful,
  I know that full well.

My frame was not hidden from you
   when I was made in the secret place.
When I was woven together in the depths of the earth,
   your eyes saw my unformed body.
All the days ordained for me
   were written in your book
   before one of them came to be.

How precious to me are your thoughts, O God!
   How vast is the sum of them!
Were I to count them,
   they would outnumber the grains of sand.
When I awake,
   I am still with you.

      . . .

Search me, O God, and know my heart;
   test me and know my anxious thoughts.
See if there is any offensive way in me,
   and lead me in the way everlasting.
              —Psalm 139:1–18, 23–24 (NIV)

→≫ ≪←

Dear God,
   I thank you for being with me in this
important—and difficult—responsibility
of motherhood.
              Amen ৵

→≫ Part II ≪←
Oh Where, Oh Where Has My Sanity Gone?
The Side Effects of Motherhood

Oh where, oh where has my sanity gone?
Oh where, oh where can it be?
With its smiling face and undaunted grace,
Oh where, oh where can it be? ≥∾

→≫ 4 ≪←
The Cost of the Treasure

So Jesus went back with them to Nazareth, where he was obedient to them. His mother treasured all these things in her heart. Jesus grew both in body and in wisdom, gaining favor with God and men.

—Luke 2:51–52 (GNB)

→≫ ≪←

Oh, I've heard the sayings about money: "Money can't buy happiness" and "Money can't buy love." But I challenge you to raise a child without it. And a challenge it would be.

When my children were but a twinkle in my eye and nowhere else, I naively used financial arguments to convince my husband that we should start our family.

"How much could a little baby cost?" I asked him. "I'll nurse the baby, so we won't need to buy food for at least six months. And then when the baby does start eating, why, he certainly won't eat very much. We'll need a few clothes, and a crib, and of course some diapers. See there? Food, clothing, and shelter. What more could there be?"

As you could guess, reality hit hard when my children came along. First came the hidden costs. The obvious costs were close behind.

1. Food: I was pregnant, and then nursing two babies, so I needed more to eat. I also needed breastpads to catch the milk that leaked at inopportune times. Then when the boys started eating table food, my carefully planned meals with exact portions for two were no longer appropriate.

2. Shelter: My frugal husband and I could no longer leave our thermostat set at fifty-five, and we needed storm windows on the babies' room. Of course, the nursery had to be decorated, too: a nice paint job and some crib bumper pads and sheets and mattress pads, with wall hangings and mobiles for stimulation—at the least.

3. Clothing: Maternity clothing stores certainly take full advantage of their widening clientele. Then there's baby's clothing: how an outfit made of material measured by the square inch can be

10

as expensive as an outfit that's five times bigger is beyond me. And to realize that baby will only be wearing that outfit for several months. Next, there are children's shoes. . . .

4. Toys: Toys, toys, and more toys!

5. Doctors' bills: Well-baby checkups, sick visits, vaccinations, and medicine. And that's if all goes routinely.

6. Services: babysitters, mothers'-morning-out programs, preschool programs, daycare, swimming lessons, ballet lessons, entertainment, and birthday parties.

American Demographics (January, 1990) calculated that the average cost of the goods and services a baby consumes during its first year (not counting delivery expenses) is $5,774. The article also quotes the U.S. Department of Agriculture's estimate that the total cost of raising a child is $100,000.[7] And after that comes college!

Certainly there are ways to cut down on those costs: breastfeeding instead of formula, cloth diapers instead of disposables, hand-me-down and consignment store clothing, borrowed baby equipment, and so forth. I'm often amused—even in myself—at the items that parents are convinced that they *need.* I was speaking with a mother-to-be recently who was searching for a fitted sheet for her bassinet mattress—a larger sheet folded over the mattress just wouldn't do.

But even for the most frugal parents, some costs are unavoidable. I guess you could say that money is a necessary evil in raising a child. But the money buys the "things" for the child—it doesn't buy the love. The money helps you meet the child's physical needs—it doesn't buy the happiness.

In fact, the best moments in preschool motherhood are absolutely free. You feel the softness of Baby Lisa's skin and the warmth and closeness of her body; you hear the little sounds of contentment as she snuggles down in your arms to eat. You see the pleasure on Mikey's face when he presents you with the dandelions and feathers, and you know he thought of you when he chose his gifts. You gaze on your children's peaceful faces as they sleep, and thank God for such special, unequaled gifts. You listen to the melody of their laughter and the childish lyrics as they talk. And you hug and soothe a hurt child, as you ache for the hurt but are grateful you can be there to comfort.

Mary had the right idea as she looked upon her son Jesus. I like the word "treasure" that the translators* used in Luke 2:51. What better treasures do we as mothers have than thoughts of our children, than time with our children, than our children themselves? What houses, jewelry, clothes, or vacations can compare?

We must use some money for the upkeep of our treasures, but our treasures themselves are priceless. As we watch our children grow in body and in wisdom, we can savor the love and the happiness that such treasures bring. ❧

*Both the Good News Bible and the New International Version chose the verb "treasure" to describe how Mary thought of Jesus' boyhood.

⇢⟫ 5 ⟪⇠
Unsolicited Advice, Unwelcome Comments

The time came for Elizabeth to have her baby, and she gave birth to a son. Her neighbors and relatives heard how wonderfully good the Lord had been to her, and they all rejoiced with her.

When the baby was a week old, they came to circumcise him, and they were going to name him Zechariah, after his father. But his mother said, "No! His name is to be John."

They said to her, "But you don't have any relative with that name!" Then they made signs to his father, asking him what name he would like the boy to have.

Zechariah asked for a writing pad and wrote, "His name is John." How surprised they all were! At that moment Zechariah was able to speak again, and he started praising God.

—Luke 1:57–64 (RSV)

As you can see, unsolicited advice about children is nothing new. The advice begins flowing freely when a woman becomes pregnant: "Don't raise your arms above your head, dearie, or the cord will wrap itself around the baby." It reaches a peak soon after the baby is born: "Now don't you go picking up that baby every time it cries or you'll spoil it" and "Remember to put a sweater and hat on the baby when you take him outside," after which you may hear "Don't overdress that baby or he'll get too hot." One helpful Heloise may chastise you for not putting the baby on an eating schedule, while someone else may scold you for not feeding the baby often enough.

When my twins were infants, I became acquainted with a story of a woman who took her baby for a walk in the city. She dutifully put on the baby's cap and began her trek. She was soon greeted by a woman who insisted that the child must be burning up under such cover on such a warm day. The mother took the cap off. Next she was stopped by a woman exclaiming how the baby would catch cold if he weren't more warmly dressed. The mother put the cap back on. I'm sure you can guess what the next piece of unsolicited advice was. I don't remember exactly where the cap was by time the mother and baby returned from their walk, but I do know that it was where the *mother* wanted it.

Soon after that, I took my four-month-old twins to the grocery store on an unseasonably warm February day. Yes, it was February, but it was warm enough for my babies to go without hats. The stranger in the parking lot did not agree, and she made sure I knew her opinion.

Public comments are more than doubled when twins are involved. I would have to plan for at least an extra half hour on all my outings with my newborn twins to compensate for the question-and-answer sessions. That extra half hour, of course, didn't count the normal baby needs for outings: changes, feedings, soothings, and so forth. As any mother can appreciate, "running errands" took on a whole new meaning.

As a mother of twins, I began to prepare for the frequent comment, "double trouble." I started my own list of responses: "double blessings" or "double fun" or "double joy." Even if I didn't feel that way at the time, I knew it was what my boys needed to hear. I also established my stock response to the comment "Glad it's you and not me." "Me, too," I would reply. I knew that the well-intentioned comments needed to be sifted through the sieve of my children's needs.

Advice slows down a bit as the baby becomes a toddler and then a preschooler, but hot spots remain: feeding—what, how much, and how; toilet-training—how and when; discipline—to spank or not to spank. A working mother can face comments that wound, usually from people who don't know the situation or reasons. And a mother who chooses to stay at home can also feel the disapproval of others.

Unsolicited advice can be unsettling, for a first-time mother especially. Although gems of wisdom may be found within the words of advice, the new mother may not have enough confidence in her own knowledge and abilities to subtly shake away the chaff as she keeps the grain.

Oscar Wilde once said, "I always pass on good advice. It is the only thing to do with it. It is never any use to oneself" (*An Ideal Husband,* 1895). Although I wouldn't go to that extreme, it is important to remember that the advice and comments must be sifted and sorted, and that you must decide what applies to you and your child, and what is of no use. What worked for Friendly

Fran and her family might not work for you. Only you know your child, yourself, and your situation.

The advisors are well-meaning, and sometimes they are correct. As an advisee, you can listen to their words and weigh them. All of us as mothers can learn from one another. However, you may need to stand firm in decisions you have made. If you feel as though your decisions are informed ones, made with God's guidance and wisdom, then you can politely smile at any conflicting advice.

Zechariah and Elizabeth got much advice about their son's name. But these two followers of God knew that their Lord wanted the baby to be named "John." They stood firm, and God blessed them. ૄ

Your Eroding Talents

. . . "Once there was a man who was about to leave home on a trip; he called his servants and put them in charge of his property. He gave to each one according to his ability: to one he gave five thousand gold coins, to another he gave two thousand, and to another he gave one thousand. Then he left on his trip. The servant who had received five thousand coins went at once and invested his money and earned another five thousand. . . . After a long time the master of those servants came back and settled accounts with them. The servant who had received five thousand coins came in and handed over the other five thousand. 'You gave me five thousand coins, sir,' he said. 'Look! Here are another five thousand that I have earned.' 'Well done, you good and faithful servant!' said his master. 'You have been faithful in managing small amounts, so I will put you in charge of large amounts. Come on in and share my happiness!'"

—Matthew 25:14–16, 19–21 (GNB)
→≫ ≪←

My sister, mother of two, has an apron that asks, "For this I spent four years in college?" I sometimes look around at my domestic duties—laundry, dishes, bathrooms, dusting—and wonder, *What's the good of my B.A. now?*

It's not my college degree I regret. The intellectual stimulation and challenge I received are irreplaceable. It's the thought that I studied British literature—only to read A.A. Milne's *Winnie the Pooh.* I learned of American literature—that I might read Dr. Seuss's *Hop on Pop.* I was a student of creative writing—so I could fill out my children's preschool registration forms. I took theatre courses—and I pretend I'm Bambi's mama. I studied astrophysics—and I recite, "Star light, star bright, first star I see tonight. I wish I may, I wish I might, have the wish I wish tonight." I took psychology courses—but I still don't understand my children.

I have the fear that by the time I once again have the opportunity to receive sufficient intellectual stimulation, my brain wrinkles will have smoothed out like a pebble in a brook. Already I'm afraid to mingle with a group involved in an erudite discussion. I know I would show my rustiness or make an embarrassing blunder: "But Mr. Rogers says . . . !"

One of the Adams women, Elizabeth Shaw, sister-in-law to President John Adams, came to my rescue, assuring me I was not alone.

> Elizabeth often deplored how intellectually enervating a woman's domestic tasks could be, particularly after offspring arrived. . . . "For if ideas present themselves to my mind," Elizabeth lamented, "it is too much like the good seed sown among thorns. They are soon erased and swallowed up by the cares of the world, the noise and wants of my family and children. . . . I am almost sometimes mentally starved."[8]

The demands of motherhood can be so consuming that little time or energy is left for anything else. Whatever a woman's other love may be—reading, writing, playing tennis, sewing, decorating, exercising—this love may be pushed aside in the attempt to keep up with kids and husband and house. Madeleine L'Engle, author of *A Wrinkle in Time* and a multitude of other books, wrote,

> I was struggling to write, to keep house, help in the store, be a good mother, and yet improve my skills as a storyteller. And that decade was one of rejection slips. I would mutter as I cleaned the house, "Emily Bronte didn't have to run the vacuum cleaner. Jane Austen didn't do the cooking."[9]

Making the time to keep active and skilled in your hobbies and talents can help you control your stress level. Not making the time can be a frustration. The most important "talents" or "gold coins" you have been given now are your relationships with God, with your husband, and with your children. You must put your best efforts into managing these gifts. But the servant who received five talents from the master (King James Version of the parable) didn't invest three of them only—he invested all five.

Making the effort to use all your talents may cause conflict, too. Perhaps if you take time to participate in your favorite activity, you will return to find that your kids have trashed the house, dirtied more dishes, and otherwise extended your "to do" list. Your husband may not be pleased about keeping the kids, or you may have to find a sitter.

The result, however, is worth the effort for all involved. Your husband, your children, and you will be better off with a saner, more fulfilled you. Whatever you value of yourself, keep that intact. If you value your physical condition, make the time to exercise—childbearing has done enough damage to your body. If you value your abilities in a certain area, keep those talents fine-tuned—it will be a great self-esteem booster. And if you value your mental faculties, find avenues of intellectual stimulation. By the time your children become teenagers, they will be convinced that you know nothing. Make sure you don't agree with them. ટ✢

⇶ 7 ⇷
Hope for the Stick-Figure Housewife

The Lord answered her, "Martha, Martha! You are worried and troubled over so many things, but just one is needed. Mary has chosen the right thing, and it will not be taken away from her."
—Luke 10:41 (GNB)

⇶ ⇷

There are three categories of preschool mothers: (1) those who by hook or crook or broom or brush still manage to keep their houses neat and clean; (2) those who have houses that look as though one of its members must be a miniature whirlwind, but they make no apologies for it; and (3) those of us who greet a guest at the door with "Come on in, but please ignore the mess! I just straightened up last week but you certainly can't tell, I know. Oops! Watch that spot on the floor or you may never come unglued. Oh, I'm sorry. Jimmy! I told you to pick up those marbles! Here, let me just move these blocks out of the way and you can sit down on the sofa. So. How are things with you?"

The preschool mother who maintains an orderly house, seemingly with a natural effort, is like a master artist who has the talent, the knowledge, and the will to create a work of art under her roof. She paints beautiful, lifelike portraits on her canvas. The rest of us lack the artistic talent, the know-how, or the self-discipline, and we end up with only stick-figure people on our paper.

Those who keep immaculate houses astound those of us who can't. At times we venerate them and are convinced that they have truly "arrived," and we long for the day when we, too, can reach that state of perfection. At our less noble times, we are convinced that not only are those women neurotic, but that they certainly must be raising neurotic, stifled children as well. At our good and bad times both, we hope that when no one is around their houses are cluttered, too. We are tempted to peek under their sofas to see if we can find toys or magazines or dustballs—but we are afraid to for fear that the hidden recesses, too, will be immaculate. We dream of dropping in on them unexpectedly and finding a toy or pillow out of place, and we conjure up visions of them sweeping crumbs under the rug when they hear the doorbell ring.

One such mythical beast is a member of my church. She has a spotless house and a perfect little girl. When she became pregnant with her second child, I secretly hoped that she would give birth to a happy, healthy, rowdy, messy boy. But, alas, her second child was a little girl who rarely cried and who slept through the night soon after birth and who puts the burp rag on her mother's shoulder herself. I console myself by thinking that the Lord must have an abundance of confidence in me to have chosen to bless me in other ways instead.

I have a print hanging in my front hall that claims that the reason that my doorbell doesn't sparkle is that I've spent so much wonderful time with my children that their eyes are sparkling instead. I'll tell you, though, there are many times when my doorbell doesn't sparkle, the house is a mess, and the dirty laundry is beginning to crawl out of place, yet I wonder where the time has gone. I don't feel that I've spent "quality time" with my children, but the house has no evidence of "quality time" either. I feel like the voodoo-cursed runner in *The World's Greatest Athlete* who is running his heart out but is getting absolutely no place at all. As my husband's grandmother used to say, I've been "turning around in circles all day."

I value a clean house, and I've heard that cleanliness is next to godliness, but I also value my children, and I know that God does, too. And though my sanity seems at times to be tied to the tidiness of my house, for the time being I have to accept the fact that *House Beautiful* will not come knocking on my door (unless they are in need of a "before" picture).

All of us in this stage of life can benefit from realizing that wonderful housekeeping is indeed an art. Any of us can draw a stick figure to represent a person, but only a few can draw beautiful, lifelike portraits. Any of us can clean a toilet and dust a bookshelf, but only a few have the mysterious and magnificent ability to create and maintain a house that is soothingly clean. If you are one of these housekeeping artists, rejoice! Thank God for blessing you with that talent! If you are a stick-figure housekeeper, take heart! Realize first that God has blessed you elsewhere! Realize next that, if it really matters to you, you can improve your artistic skills. Bookstore shelves have many books on household management that can hone your abilities.[10]

Learn, improve, pass along your newfound knowledge to your

children, but do keep your priorities in order, too. Make sure your children continue to realize that they are more important to you than a sparkling house is. Yes, the wonderful woman described in Proverbs 31 does sound like the epitome of an efficient, organized housekeeper, but if her children were old enough to "rise up and call her blessed," then she was obviously long past the preschool mother stage. ಕ್ಕಾ

⇥ 8 ⇤
Adult Conversation or Big-People Talk

Then he went back upstairs, broke bread, and ate. After talking with them for a long time, even until sunrise, Paul left.
—Acts 20:11 (GNB)

⇥ ⇤

One can only imagine what Paul and his friends talked about: the Scriptures, right and wrong, ideas and feelings, Jesus. Whatever it was that kept them talking through the night, I'm sure it was stimulating and challenging. Stimulating and challenging. Those are two words that I would not use to describe many of my conversations of late.

My college roommate dropped by a few evenings ago. We chatted as she jiggled her fussing four-month-old baby—the baby bounce at which all new mothers quickly become proficient. It was tough to carry on a serious conversation—I felt as if I was talking to one of those dashboard dogs with a spring in his neck.

Serious conversation is frequently difficult—or seemingly nonexistent—for many a preschool mother. Imagine watching "Sesame Street," reading Dr. Seuss, and listening to a Mother Goose tape, and then trying to discuss politics or theology. "Dukakis could never have made a good president—he looks too much like Ernie," or "I think we need to be persistent in our prayers, like that fellow in *Green Eggs and Ham.*" It's like a writer trying to write for "I Love Lucy" in the morning and *The Wall Street Journal* in the afternoon.

My husband praises me for taking an interest in his work. Yes, I think it's an important spousal duty, and his job does interest me, but my motives are not purely unselfish. I value the excitement that I feel when my mind starts functioning again, when the cobwebs and mush start draining out, and I realize that I have not lost all of the abilities I was so keenly aware of in my college days.

(Sidenote: Have you heard the old wives' tale that a woman loses more brain cells with each child she bears? On some days I feel as though that's the only logical explanation for families with more than one child.)

These intelligent exchanges, however, are hampered by another obstacle: interruptions. I'd like to see two professors trying to discuss their disciplines during their coffee break if they were constantly being interrupted by Mommy-this or Daddy-that. Not only is the train of thought hard to follow, but the feelings and passions involved are hard to maintain. A woman baring her soul to her friend may find it hard to continue after answering her daughter's "Mommy, I have to poop. Come help me." A preschool mother may find that the number of main topics she discusses dwindles as well. Throw two mothers together and what will they probably discuss? The kids. Throw mom and dad together and what will they often discuss? Right. How many of you have gotten a night out, with just your spouse, and what did you talk about? Exactly.

Brains of mush; trains of thought that have jumped the track; one-track minds: preschool parents face many barriers to communication. Yet communication is important.

After Jesus had left the followers on the road to Emmaus, "They said to each other, 'Wasn't it like a fire burning in us when he talked to us on the road and explained the Scriptures to us?' " (Luke 24:32, GNB). We need to take the time to study the Bible, to pray, and to talk our ideas and convictions out with Christian friends. We must take the opportunity to share our feelings, good and bad, with others.

An essential and urgent solution for parents is to find time alone. It must be more than just five minutes while the kids are occupied elsewhere, to allow for the necessary shifting of gears. It must be without interruption to maintain the thoughts and passions. It must be on "other" subjects to remind us that we are individuals, and husband and wife, not just parents.

No, big people talk isn't all gone, Sweetie. Don't cry, Mommy make it all better. Atta girl. Give Mommy kiss. Bye-bye! ๖

➤➤ 9 ◄◄

First Children of the Furry Variety

Then God said, "And now we will make human beings; they will be like us and resemble us. They will have power over the fish, the birds, and all animals, domestic and wild, large and small."
—Genesis 1:26 (GNB)

➤➤ ◄◄

Soon after I became pregnant the first time around, a friend of my husband's shared with us these words of wisdom out of his own experience: "Don't expect," he warned us, "that you will be as crazy about your dog after your baby is born as you are now. Your focus will change entirely." I nodded politely and filed the comment away in my "that-could-never-happen-to-me" file. Certainly I would love my child, but nothing could ever detract from my relationship with my wonderful little puppy dog. I read all the "Preparing Your Pet for the New Arrival" articles as faithfully as I would the "Preparing Your Child for the New Little Sibling" articles two years later. We had our strategies all worked out, including: (1) "make sure you pay attention to your pet while the baby is around, so the pet won't associate the presence of the baby with lack of attention," and (2) Lewwy was to bring the babies into the house when I first came home from the hospital so I could adequately greet my canine friend after my extended absence.

The big day arrived; the twins and I were to come home from the hospital and we would become a happy family of five. In our preparations to leave the hospital, I nursed the boys, got them dressed, got myself dressed, and ate my final hospital meal, as Lewwy took two cartloads of suitcases, formula samples, and flowers to the car, loaded the paraphernalia, and figured out the car seats. We bundled up the twins for the cold November weather, took lots of pictures, and answered all the people exclaiming "Are they twins?" By the time we finally made it to the car, it was feeding time again, but we would not be diverted from our purpose (besides which we had left my hospital room and so had no private place to take care of such business), so we had our first stereo-crying car ride.

I'm sure that by this point in my narrative, your mind has been diverted from the subject of my dog. So had mine. I might have given her a sweet little "Hello, Sandy girl. Did you miss me?" as I rushed by to get positioned to feed the babies. There went strategy number two.

There was another major obstacle to my continued relationship with my doggie that I had never considered: clean hands. As a paranoid, well-taught new mother, I spent much time washing my hands, making sure they were flawlessly clean before I touched my newborns. So now, as one who was already nervous, exhausted, and hormonally-imbalanced, and who had already washed her hands a dozen times that day, I had no desire to pat my puppy dog and guarantee another hand-washing before I could pick up a needy baby. There went strategy number one.

It was all downhill from there. My time and attention were demanded by my babies. My maternal need to nurture was fully filled by my two new responsibilities. My love was given freely to them and diverted from my puppy. My dog got "put in her place" as a pet, rather than a peer. She became just another item on my too-long "to do" list.

My husband found a letter I had written him long before the children were born when I had had to be out of town for a while. I closed with "P.S. Give Sandy a big hug for me." He also reminded me that I had insisted upon giving Sandy a good rubdown every evening before bed. I believed him only because he is not a liar. I have little memory of those days and that part of my relationship with my dog.

Me. The same person who had wanted to be a veterinarian when I grew up, who had been crushed by the thought that animals might not be with us in heaven. Many people do manage to maintain their attachment to their pet, but not I. Our friend was right, and yes, it happened to me. My focus changed.

Before motherhood, a woman has no idea of what a time-consuming responsibility she will be assuming. No one can adequately prepare her for the change in her lifestyle. Yet the changes are made abruptly; priorities are rearranged; and there is a new dimension to the word "love." ઙ

⇢≫ Part III ≪⇠
Simple Simon Had a Baby:
Raising Your Child with Wisdom

Simple Simon met a pieman
   Going to the fair;
Says Simple Simon to the pieman,
   Let me taste your ware.

Says the pieman to Simple Simon,
   Show me first your penny;
Says Simple Simon to the pieman,
   Indeed I have not any.

Simple Simon went a-fishing
   For to catch a whale;
All the water he had got
   Was in his mother's pail.

Now Simple Simon had a baby,
   And knew that it should grow,
So he sprinkled water and fertilizer
   From its head to the tip of its toe.

The baby cried—he gave it a steak—
   It cried and he gave it root beer;
The baby pouted and Simon shouted
   Words of logic and sensible cheer.[11] ɛ✺

⇉ 10 ⇇

Parental Objectives

If you dig a pit, you fall in it; if you break through a wall, a snake bites you. If you work in a stone quarry, you get hurt by stones. If you split wood, you get hurt doing it. If your ax is dull and you don't sharpen it, you have to work harder to use it. It is smarter to plan ahead. Knowing how to charm a snake is of no use if you let the snake bite first. . . . No one knows what is going to happen next, and no one can tell us what will happen after we die.

—*Ecclesiastes 10:8–11, 14b (GNB)*
⇉ ⇇

To be a teacher these days, you must acknowledge, understand, and utilize the principle of "educational objectives": putting on paper the skills your students are to master and exactly how you will teach them these skills.

To the chagrin of many a teacher, however, these objectives must often be quite detailed:

Objective

Students must be able to use scissors to cut out a square that has been drawn on a piece of paper.

Method

—Students will learn to insert their thumbs and pointer fingers into the holes in the scissors and to hold the scissors correctly. I will demonstrate the correct positioning and then help them to insert their own fingers.

—They will learn to move the blades back and forth by moving the thumb and pointer finger apart and together in an even motion. I will demonstrate the correct movement and then help them to move the blades by themselves.

—Students will learn to use the scissors to cut paper. They will be given opportunities in class to practice this skill on various types of paper.

—They will learn to be able to cut along lines that have been predrawn onto the paper. They will be given opportunities to practice many times to improve the skill level.

Standard of Measurement

Each student must cut a square out of a piece of paper along the lines drawn on that paper. In order for the task to be accomplished in an acceptable manner, no cut must be more than ten degrees off the line that was drawn.

As a budding teacher, I balked at the busywork involved in putting together such a detailed list of purposes and procedures. I was also one of those that hated to have to "show my work" in my high school geometry and algebra classes. I figured as long as I knew how to get from point A to point Z in my head and understood the underlying concept, why should I put all the repetitious steps down on paper?

Eventually, however, I came to appreciate the essence and concept behind the principle: as the saying goes, if you don't know where you're going, you'll probably end up somewhere else (and probably someplace you'd rather not be). Putting onto paper the goals and the steps in achieving them does give a clear idea of what needs to be done, ultimately and in the interim.

As parents, however, we have no "head of the department" or school principal standing over us forcing us to write down our objectives, our methods, or our standards of measurement. Most of us have these nebulous ideas in our heads about what we want our children to be like when they grow up, but rarely do we verbalize these ideas or even think about them to such an extent that they become concrete rather than abstract.

Just as a teacher's educational objectives can assist in teaching, a parent's parental objectives can assist in parenting. If you, as a parent, can examine what you really want for your children, can be aware of the best way to get from here to there, and then can consciously attempt to follow that course, your children will be more likely to reach those objectives.

For example, one objective that my mother held for each of her children was that we would find suitable Christian marriage partners. As part of her strategy, she prayed regularly for the spouses that my sister, my brother, and I would ultimately choose. And before my mother died, each child had married a loving and mature Christian partner.

I continue my mother's practice for my own children. When I pray for my children's future spouses, I know that God hears and blesses my prayer and works in the minds and hearts of my own children that they may be able to make the right choice when it comes. Perhaps God works in the minds and hearts of those future wives and that future husband as well. At that very moment, however, God noticeably works in my mind and heart, reminding me of the importance of the relationship between my husband and myself. If our children see that husbands and wives respect each other and treat each other with dignity and pride and love, then they will look for partners who will treat them like that. If our children see that marriage takes commitment as well as love, effort as well as joy, if they see marriage as a mixture of patience and praise, time and growth, communication and laughter, then they will expect no less from themselves in their own union under the Lord. Thus, my prayer—my goal—reminds me of a method I need to use in achieving an important objective for my children.

Another regular prayer I have for my children is that they acquire the fruits of the Spirit: "But the Spirit produces love, joy, peace, patience, kindness, goodness, faithfulness, humility, and self-control" (Galatians 5: 20–22, GNB). I know that God blesses my prayer not only by working in my children but also by refocusing my objectives and methods.

For example, suppose one night I prayed for Brian:

Lord, please bless Brian with the fruits of your Spirit. Give him love, grant him joy. . . Hmm, I missed an opportunity today to show Brian that joy can come even in the midst of trouble. I know he was upset that we couldn't take a picnic because of the rain. We could have talked about joy in the Lord not being dependent upon circumstances. I could have helped him see that our beach blanket picnic on the family room floor was fun, too, and that good things can come in spite of problems. I'll have to talk with Brian about that tomorrow. God, give Brian peace, in all circumstances; give him patience, kindness, goodness. Ah! Goodness! That's an area I've really seen growth in. I remember that used to be the fruit that would stop me quick every time I prayed for him. I'll need to affirm Brian in that area. Thanks, Lord, for that growth. Help me to be aware of how we can continue it.

And so on. Every prayer is different, but every prayer helps me to regain my sense of direction.

In addition, this prayer reminds me of my number one goal for my children: in order for them to fully have the fruits of the Spirit, they need to have God's Spirit in their lives—they need to accept Jesus as their Savior. So I renew my objectives to teach them of God's love and plan for them.

In choosing a Scripture reference for this chapter, the passage in Ecclesiastes that suggests "it is smarter to plan ahead" won hands down over the verse in Proverbs that admonishes to "plan carefully what you do, and whatever you do will turn out right" (Proverbs 4:26, GNB). I didn't feel comfortable with the proverb's guarantee that everything would turn out right. We all know that for parents there is no guarantee that even our best plans and actions and intentions will turn out a perfect adult in eighteen years.

I'm a real fan of Ecclesiastes. To me, that book is like the Murphy's Laws of the Bible. The writer of Ecclesiastes is a lot more cynical than the writer of Proverbs, but most of us have experienced and seen enough to be wary of the blanket promises that many of the proverbs seem to contain. Obviously, the intent of the proverbs is absolutely correct. As James Dobson explains in *Parenting Isn't for Cowards,* Solomon's sayings are meant as "probabilities," not "promises," which convey the writer's "divinely inspired observations on the way human nature and God's universe work."[12] Obviously, any time human beings are involved in a situation, very little is absolute. We can plan carefully what we do, as Proverbs 4:26 suggests, but there's no guarantee that it will turn out right, although planning will increase our odds greatly.

The writer of Ecclesiastes, however, has seen the confusing and depressing sides of life. "The Philosopher tried to find comforting words, but the words he wrote were honest" (Ecclesiastes 12:10, GNB). Yet the conclusion is the foundation on which we can build our hopes and goals:

> After all this, there is only one thing to say: Have reverence for God, and obey his commands, because this is all that man was created for. God is going to judge everything we do, whether good or bad, even things done in secret *(Ecclesiastes 12: 13–14, GNB).*

If the writer of Ecclesiastes had been thinking about children when writing the passage on planning ahead, I believe the verses would have ended up a bit more like this:

31

If you buy a sandbox for your child, you will get sand thrown at you; if you manage to get your child enrolled in just the right preschool, he will cry miserably each morning when you drop him off. If you take years away from your professional career to stay home and raise your kids, one of them will ask you, "Hey, Mom, why don't you do anything exciting, like being a newscaster like Drew's mom?" If you cook all of your family's meals to save on the budget and to insure adequate nutrition, you will burn your finger and hear a child ask, "Meatloaf again?" If your mind is dull from reading recipes, bills, and books with all one-syllable words, you will have to work harder to use it. It is smarter to plan ahead. Knowing how to raise a child is of no use if you let the child bite you first. . . . No one knows what stage your children are going to go through next, and no one can tell you what will happen after they leave home.

Yet the philosopher would not have left it at that.

Have reverence for God, obey his commands, and teach your children to do the same, for this is what we all were created for. Yes, God is going to judge the bad things we do, but don't forget—God will judge the good, too! ॐ

⇾⟫ 11 ⟪⇽
Parenting Strategies 101: Objectives

Train up a child in the way he should go,
and when he is old he will not depart from it.
—*Proverbs 22:6 (RSV)*

⇾⟫ ⟪⇽

I like that word "train." It emphasizes the importance of parenting, an importance that is often overlooked. The word "raise" is too nebulous, allowing parents to believe they are competent if they simply clothe and feed the child, send him to school, and put out "fires" as they occur. But "training" evokes more active pictures: of a trainer teaching the boxer all the right moves and encouraging him as he practices; of a horse trainer putting the mount through the gaits and striving towards perfection; of a teacher imparting skills and knowledge needed by students for future jobs; of a sergeant urging recruits to strengthen endurance so that they will be prepared for battle.

So, Mom, you see that your job as a trainer is really pretty important. Keep that in mind as we move on.

As your child's trainer, you must first know where he or she should go—your objectives. In addition, you must separate the essential values from the unessential ones. How many of the ideas that we as parents have in our heads are really not important, or are not our decisions to make? "My son needs to be strong and athletic." "I want my daughter to be prettier than other girls." "I'd like Sally to be a doctor or lawyer." "Chris should be sociable and outgoing." "My child should be popular." The Bible is full of essential values for all of us: love, joy, peace, patience, kindness, goodness, gentleness, self-control, wisdom, honesty, humility, and so on.

Keep in mind, of course, that there are goals that can fall between the two extremes of essential and unessential. These can still be parental objectives, but you must be careful that your child realizes that they are optional and, just like with the other objectives, you will love him or her even if the objectives are not attained. You may desire that Tommy will enjoy music as much as you do, or that Sally will enjoy sports. Once you've identified these goals, you can provide the opportunities for these goals to be met. Take Tommy to the symphony and sign Sally up for t-ball. Buy Tommy a copy of *Peter and the Wolf* and buy Sally a Nerf football. However, if Tommy insists that an opera sounds like a pasture full of dying cows and Sally says that the only good pitcher is a pitcher of lemonade, then back off.

What goals do you have for your children? Use the chart on page 36 to examine your parental objectives. First, brainstorm and list all of the traits, values, and goals in each category that you desire for each child. Of course, many of the goals will be the same for more than one child. If you and your husband each fill out a chart and then compare goals, you will probably find many items that need discussion, since each parent approaches the goals from a different perspective.

Now that you've listed some of your priorities for your children, weed through what you wrote down. Are there objectives that really are not essential goals? For example, are you hoping your child will be good-looking and famous? Do you desire that your child will be wealthy? (It would be nice to be able to live off your kids for a while, though, wouldn't it?) Are there objectives that are too specific, not leaving your child room for his or her own decisions? For example, are you too specific on the type of career your child will have? Are there objectives that you may not have the right to decide, realizing that your child is different from you and has his or her own personality and interests? Are you insistent, for example, that your child will be able to play the pan flute like Zamfir, will be both a running back and an outfielder like Bo Jackson, or will be a great conductor like Leonard Bernstein?

Now that you've weeded those out, circle the objectives that you feel are essential and undeniable. Post these objectives where you can be reminded of them frequently: on your bathroom mirror or over the kitchen sink.

My primary parental objectives are summed up in Ephesians 3: 14–21 (GNB):

> For this reason I fall on my knees before the Father, from whom every family in heaven and on earth receives its true name. I ask God from the wealth of his glory to give you power through his Spirit to be strong in your inner selves, and I pray that Christ will make his home in your hearts through faith. I pray that you may have your

roots and foundation in love, so that you, together with all God's people, may have the power to understand how broad and long, how high and deep, is Christ's love. Yes, may you come to know his love—although it can never be fully known—and so be completely filled with the very nature of God.

To him who by means of his power working in us is able to do so much more than we can ever ask for, or even think of: to God be the glory in the church and in Christ Jesus for all time, forever and ever! Amen. ≥•

My Goals for My Children

Category	Child 1:	Child 2:	Child 3:
Spiritual			
Emotional			
Physical			
Values			
Social/ Friendships			
Marital			
Career			
Family			
Other hopes			

→》》 12 《《←
Parenting Strategies 201: How-tos

Being wise is better than being strong; yes, knowledge is more important than strength. After all, you must make careful plans before you fight a battle, and the more good advice you get, the more likely you are to win.

—Proverbs 24:5–6 (GNB)

→》》 《《←

Now you know where you're going, and you're ready to pull out the map and figure out how to get there, remembering that there may be many detours along the way.

One of my detours arose in the county of Spiritual Objectives. In mapping out my trip, I decided to use the Scripture Memorization Highway to take my children to the town of Know-Your-Bible. Accordingly, I chose a simple Scripture verse for my three-year old twins—not too simple, though, for I knew that my intelligent children were capable of more than "Jesus wept." Our first verse was Ephesians 6:1: "Children, obey your parents. This is the right thing to do" *(The Living Bible).*

I very patiently gathered my boys on my lap and explained to them what we were going to do. As they squirmed and wiggled, they raised no objections, so I proceeded to step two.

"Okay, boys. Listen. 'Children, obey your parents. This is the right thing to do.' Ephesians 6:1. 'Children, obey your parents. This is the right thing to do.' Okay, now you try. 'Children, obey your parents.' Say that. 'Children, obey your parents.' "

" 'Children,' " mumbled a squirming Brian.

"Good! Very good, Brian! Now Daniel, 'Children, obey your parents.' "

" 'Children!' "

"Very good, Daniel! 'Children.' Now the next part: 'obey your parents.' Daniel, come back up here. 'Obey your parents.' Say that, boys."

"Mommy, I want a snack."

"No, it's not snack time right now. Say the Bible verse, Brian. 'Obey your parents.' "

" 'Obey your parents!' " Daniel proclaimed triumphantly.

"Yay, Daniel! 'Obey your parents.' Brian, can you say that?"

"No!" he managed to say between sobs. "I want a snack!"

"In a little bit, sweetie. You know we just finished lunch."

"I want a snack!"

"Later. (Sigh!) Daniel, try this next part. 'This is the right thing to do.' Daniel, stop rolling on the floor, please. Did you hear me? Say this: 'This is the right thing to do.' "

" 'This is the . . . .' "

" 'This is the right thing to do.' "

" 'This is the, uh, the funny thing to do!' "

"Tee-hee-hee!" Brian giggled in response.

"Yeah!" Daniel exclaimed. "This is the funny thing to do!"

"No, boys, let's be serious now. The Bible verse says, 'This is the right thing to do.' "

"This is the funny thing to do!" Brian yelled.

"This is the funny thing to do! This is the funny thing to do!"

By this time both boys were bouncing off the sofa, yelling their newly learned Scripture verse and giggling as they bounced.

"This is the funny thing to do!"

So my first major attempt at a concrete spiritual objective was a flop. Even when I tried again the next day with a different verse, they remembered the hilarity of the previous day and behaved the same way. I knew I'd have to wait till memories faded and maturity increased.

The paraphrase of Bobby Burns' words was right: "The best laid plans of mice and men go oft awry." And with that warning, Parenting 201: How-tos, can proceed.

Mommy/Trainer, you know your objectives. Now how do you reach them? Though your plans may "go oft awry," you must plan nonetheless. And your strategies can come from several sources.

Most importantly, you can glean much wisdom and guidance as you study God's Word and as you pray. Being the best parent you can be demands much prayer for wisdom in knowing how to deal with your children and handle the problems and stages that arise.

Listen to what is wise and try to understand it. Yes, beg for knowledge; plead for insight. Look for it as hard as you would for silver or some hidden treasure. If you do, you will know what it means to fear the Lord and you will succeed in learning about God. It is the Lord who gives wisdom; from him come knowledge and understanding *(Proverbs 2:2–6, GNB)*.

You learned a lot about parenting while you were a child. Remember saying, "I'll never do that to my kids"? Go back to your childhood memories. Perhaps you really had spotted a weakness in your parents' parenting skills when you made that statement, and you can avoid that fault now that you are the parent. Or perhaps now you laugh and realize that your parents were right all along. Either way, you can learn a lot from your own experiences.

Similarly, you can learn from other parents and from applying your own common sense. Oftentimes other parents have gone through similar situations and have learned tricks of the trade that they're willing to share.

Your child did not come equipped with an owner's manual (not to mention a money-back guarantee), but with care and prayer and consideration, you can find many books to help you plan out your strategies. The publishing world now includes many Christian publishers, who are as committed to providing biblical guidance as they are to making profits. I have read and re-read many books and have profited from columns and features in Christian magazines. The books and articles have trained me as the trainer of my children by helping me to find the strategies and plans and methods that will work for me. As I've read, I've gleaned bits and pieces here and there; I've rejected some ideas and embraced others. I've learned what to do and what not to do. I've learned of my own weaknesses and of chinks in my own parenting armor.

A major problem of parenting, however, is finding the time to learn how to do it properly. By the time you hit the bed at night, you're too tired to pick up a book. And if you do pick up a book, you may not want to read about the very thing that has made you so exhausted. However, time studying parenting techniques is time well spent. How many of us would try to put together a bicycle without following an instruction booklet or without prior training in mechanics? If reading parenting books is difficult for you, however, you could try an alternative.

Perhaps several parents could form a preschool playgroup. Each week one parent could lead a discussion on a parenting book or article. Better yet, maybe you could meet at your church and the youth group would volunteer to baby-sit.

Another distinct difficulty of parenting is that your subjects can be so fickle. You may develop a wonderful strategy, and then your child has the nerve to change. Your wonderful strategy may need to be adapted, or you may need to add a new one. Trouble signs often come as children go through stages or as they try to adapt to changes in their own environment. I knew that the writer of Proverbs really meant what he said in chapter 22, verse 3, when he repeated himself word for word in chapter 27, verse 12: "Sensible people will see trouble coming and avoid it, but an unthinking person will walk right into it and regret it later" (GNB). One of my boys had been going through a period of being more sensitive and moody than usual. I had to write myself a note and place it on the kitchen table to remind myself to "give Daniel extra doses of love and hugs." (What will I do when he learns to read my notes?)

To add to the parent's frustration, the "perfect strategy" for child number one may prove worthless as you train child number two.

Proverbs 22:6 (GNB) says: "Teach a child how he should live, and he will remember it all his life." As you implement that verse, though, remember that it is not meant as a guarantee. Dobson in *Parenting Isn't for Cowards* warns very strongly against believing that it is. Rebellious sons and daughters can come from the homes of godly parents. Through the ages God's sons and daughters have rebelled against divine authority because they are free to make their own decisions. Our children may rebel too.[13]

Let your paths and plans and twists and turns be directed by your heavenly Trainer:

> Trust in the LORD with all your heart,
>   and do not rely on your own insight.
> In all ways acknowledge him,
>   and he will make straight your paths.
> —*Proverbs 3:5–6 (RSV)*

You may make your plans, but God directs your actions
—*Proverbs 16: 9(GNB)* ক

⇶ 13 ⇜
Knowing Your Child

Lord, you have examined me and you know me.
You created every part of me;
you put me together in my mother's womb.
I praise you because you are to be feared;
all you do is strange and wonderful.
I know it with all my heart.
When my bones were being formed,
carefully put together in my mother's womb,
when I was growing there in secret,
you knew that I was there—
you saw me before I was born.
Examine me, O God, and know my mind;
test me, and discover my thoughts.
Find out if there is any evil in me
and guide me in the everlasting way.
  —Psalm 139:1, 13–16a, 23–24 (GNB)

⇶ ⇜

I had the opportunity in my b.c. (before children) days to teach at a private school that worked with adolescents who struggled with dyslexia. These students, although of average or above-average intelligence, had various learning disabilities that made it difficult for them to process or to retain or to repeat the information with which they were presented. All of the students had dyslexia in common, but their learning strengths and learning weaknesses varied.

In order to teach the students most effectively, the teacher had to first get to know each student's strengths and weaknesses. Once these were determined, the teacher knew not only *what* to teach the student, but *how* to teach the student. As the year progressed, the teacher could adjust the initial determinations as he or she learned more about the student.

For example, Johnny might have trouble remembering things that he hears, but can remember and understand information that he reads and sees. Charlie might need to perform an action himself, as concretely as possible, before he really understands the

41

underlying concept. Sue might have difficulty reading—even though she has an exceptional IQ—but if she hears the material, she's got it.

The teacher, then, would write the lesson on the board for Johnny and refer him to the appropriate pages of the book. Charlie would be provided with a concrete analogy of the concept and be allowed to work with that analogy. Sue would have the necessary pages of the book read aloud to her and would be given any other necessary verbal explanations.

That sounds quite complex, and it was; but it was quite rewarding to see students learning and gaining self-confidence. As involved as the school's process may sound, however, it doesn't hold a candle to the task that a parent may face.

The school worked primarily with each student's intellectual performance. A parent is concerned with a child's intellectual, emotional, physical, and spiritual health and performance. The school sought to understand the student's learning strengths and weaknesses, and to teach him or her accordingly. A parent should seek to understand the child's learning strengths and weaknesses, the emotional make-up and personality traits, the physical abilities and needs, and the spiritual questions and weaknesses—and then to parent the child accordingly. Wow! Quite a task!

Look again at the proverb:

Train up a child **in the way he should go,**
and when he is old he will not depart from it.
—*Proverbs 22:6 (RSV, author's emphasis)*

Chuck Swindoll explains that the words "in the way he should go" mean "according to that child's way." In other words, Swindoll says,

God is not saying, "Bring up a child as *you* see him." Instead, He says, "If you want your training to be godly and wise, observe your child, be sensitive and alert so as to discover *his* way, and adapt your training accordingly."[14]

Swindoll goes on to emphasize the importance of knowing your child by observing and listening, by studying actions and reactions. And all of the information that you gather is to be used in training that child. That knowledge, he warns, will demand "two exceedingly valuable ingredients: concentration and time."[15]

The God who made each of your children, who "knit" each child together in the mother's womb (Psalm 139:13, RSV), made each child different. These differences must be recognized and respected. Even my identical twin boys have differences that are distinct and important, and that affects how I train each boy.

When my twins were infants, I had this crazy, unexamined notion that I should treat them entirely equally. Because of this, I had vague feelings of guilt that kept me from holding one of the babies because I felt bad that I wasn't holding the other one, too.

Even as they grew, I felt obliged to treat them equally—with equal doses of love and attention and affection. Then I realized that such an attitude was like insisting that each child consume 1,000 calories per day, regardless of what his metabolism called for. If Daniel needed 1200 calories to remain trim but healthy and Brian needed only 800, I would be unfair to force Brian to eat the extra 200 and to deprive Daniel of the extra 200 that he needed.

Daniel does, indeed, need more cuddling and affection on an ongoing basis. Brian, on the other hand, is most pleased with what I call his special "Brian kiss": I kiss the tip of my finger and then put my finger to his cheek. Perhaps he'll grow up to be like my brother-in-law. This "romantic" man claims to have "proposed" to my sister by handing her the engagement ring still in the ring box as she was getting out of his car and saying, "Here. I guess you've been expecting this."

Children's differences surface in discipline, too. The strategies that work for one child may not be as effective with the other. Some children are barely fazed by a spanking; others are crushed by a stern look.

Knowing your child, then, can help you to plan the appropriate training, teaching, discipline, and style of showing love. In addition, says Swindoll, by knowing your child, you can help him or her to better understand himself or herself.[16]

An excellent resource in getting to know and understand your child—and yourself—is the Myers-Briggs Type Indicator. Myers-Briggs examines different aspects of an individual's personality and helps to pin down descriptions of his or her personality traits and preferences. Trained psychologists and counselors can administer the Myers-Briggs Type Indicator test to you, or you can gain a working knowledge of the system by reading a book such as *Please Understand Me: Character and Temperament Types,* by David Keirsey and Marilyn Bates, or *One of a Kind: Making the Most of Your Child's Uniqueness,* by LaVonne Neff, which examines temperament types from a Christian perspective.

For example, one of the Myers-Briggs categories labels individuals as either "thinkers" or "feelers." The thinkers tend to react according to logic and justice. The feelers react according to emotions. If you are having a talk with your two children, trying to convince them that they must stop picking on Lonesome Lilly down the street, you can apply your knowledge of personality typing and your children. Sam is primarily a thinker, so you can focus your discussion on the justice and fairness of the situation. Jessica is primarily a feeler, so you can help her to empathize with the hurt Lonesome Lilly must feel when she's teased.

I've had a good time with Myers-Briggs personality typing. If I meet someone who also knows the types, we begin to talk in letters: "Are you a P or a J?" "That was a real N thought." "You probably feel that way because you're an F." Similarly, my husband and I will sometimes watch our kids and analyze their actions. "Mmh. Does that mean Daniel is an N?"

I remind myself, though, that my children's personality types are very fluid, that they are still experimenting to find what styles fit them best. One day Brian may act like an introvert. The next day he may put on an extravert suit to see if he likes it.

I also have to be careful not to label my children and expect them to fit the resulting molds. Preschoolers, obviously, are even more difficult to label than older children. Knowing the different ways that my children may act and react, though, helps me to know what "tactics" to try. I can use my knowledge of both sides of a trait, using both elementary logic and empathy, for example, and see which strikes the chord.

A general understanding of this subject of personality typing can lead not only to a better understanding of the people around us, but also to an acceptance of their differences—so we can better appreciate them and stop trying to change what shouldn't be changed.

Another important aspect of knowing your child is being aware of basic child development so that you can have an idea of what behavior to expect from your child at various ages. A three-year-old lacks the ability to anticipate events in the distant future, so it would be difficult for him to understand that if he cleans his room every day for a month, then he would get a new bike. An eighteen-month-old lacks the understanding and self-discipline to sit quietly for long periods of time, so it would be best to avoid taking her to your hour-long committee meetings—unless you've got lots of activities for her and unless you're ready for much fidgeting and squirming (perhaps of the other committee members, as well as of your child).

Children must grow in their ability to comprehend the messages of the Christian faith as well. A preschooler can certainly comprehend the idea of Jesus loving the children, but the fact that Jesus died for the redemption of our sins will sail way over the child's head.

God knows each of us so completely that "even the hairs of your head have all been counted" (Luke 12:7a, GNB). Many of us preschool mothers are watching our hair quickly turning to gray; others of us are pulling our hair out in fits of frustration. It's helpful—and scary—to know we can pray:

> Examine me, O God, and know my mind;
> test me, and discover my thoughts.
> —*Psalm 139:23 (GNB)*

As God loves and knows us, so we ought to love **and know** our children. ও

⇶ Part IV ⇚

How Do Your Children Grow? Some Nuts and Bolts of Motherhood

Mother, Mother, tell me, Mother,
How do your children grow?
With love and hugs and discipline
And lots of time, all in a row. ❧

➤➤ 14 ◀◀

Lizard Skins

Each one should judge his own conduct. If it is good, then he can be proud of what he himself has done, without having to compare it with what someone else has done. For everyone has to carry his own load.

—*Galatians 6:4–5 (GNB)*

➤➤ ◀◀

Most of us were raised with a basic concern about what "other people" think: "Comb your hair right now! Do you want people to think you're a slob?" "That purple shirt does NOT match those pink pants! What will people think?" "Don't carry that Barbie doll, Johnny. People will think you're a sissy." "Get your feet off that table! People will think you were born in a barn!"

Until it became inconvenient: "If everyone else jumped off a bridge, would you do it, too?" It's no wonder many of us are torn between individuality and conformity.

Unfortunately, the conflict carries over to our parenting. To combat that, we as parents need to develop our own, tailor-made, lizard skins, particularly for use in public.

Think of the embarrassing times when your child misbehaves in public. A grocery store, for example, seems to be every child's favorite place to make a scene. Your child throws a temper tantrum because you won't buy a box of Teddy Tom's Toasted Tummy Ticklers. Your natural tendency is to wonder, *These people must think I'm an awful parent! Either I can't control my child or I've given birth to a little hellion.* The little old lady in the produce section may be thinking, *Well! My children never acted like that!"* (She's losing her memory in her old age.) The psychology professor at the salad bar may be thinking, *Now the technique this mother needs is. . . ."* (The rest of the sentence may or may not be worth repeating.) And the fellow preschool mother loading her five gallons of milk is thinking, *Thank goodness it's not me this time!*

At this point, you have two choices: turn red in anger at your child and embarrassment for yourself, or zip up your lizard skin and practice your own best parenting skills. If you've done your homework and developed the basic discipline strategies that best fit your child and you, then you can forget about what everyone around may think. Don't be embarrassed for yourself, because you're doing your best; and don't be embarrassed about your child—self-esteem in a child is fragile but growing, and mom's embarrassment will only hinder that growth.

Here's another potential source of embarrassment: you're getting ready for church and your four-year-old daughter comes rushing out wearing her pink polka-dot shirt, her orange plaid skirt, her red tights, and her peach dress shoes to match the peach ribbon in her hair. "Look, Mommy! I got dressed all by myself!" Your choices? March that little girl, who is so pleased at her major accomplishment, back into her room, indicating, overtly or subtly, that she's not as wonderful as she thought she was—or, pull your lizard skin out of your own drawer and be prepared to wear it all day long.

As Paul instructs us in his letter to the Galatians, we need to judge ourselves, being proud of what we do that is good, not needing to compare our conduct with someone else's. If we study God's word, pray for guidance in understanding and wisdom, do our best to follow God's will in the raising of our children, then we needn't be concerned about a stranger's gaze.

It does matter to us what other people think. But when that concern conflicts with what is best for our child, then it must take the back seat. As the writer of Proverbs reminds us, "It is dangerous to be concerned with what others think of you, but if you trust the LORD, you are safe" (Proverbs 29:25, GNB).

Actually, most of us who have "been there" know better than to judge and jump to conclusions, anyway. Fortunately, there really aren't as many "other people" in the world as we may think. ౭ఠ

Quantity/Quality

"Never forget these commands that I am giving you today. Teach them to your children. Repeat them when you are at home and when you are away, when you are resting and when you are working."

—Deuteronomy 6:6–7 (GNB)

→≫ ≪←

My husband came home one evening and I said, "Honey, I've been feeling like I really need to spend more time reading and the housework just doesn't seem to be getting done. But it's really important to me for us to spend time talking, too. I've come up with a plan. I'll set aside thirty minutes every evening so we can spend some quality time together."

The first evening arrives. "Sweetheart," I ask, after an hour of reading and an hour of housework. "Are you ready for our quality time?"

"Of course," he replies. My husband drops the sports section and Daniel runs up to me and expresses his need to go pee-pee. When that business is completed, Rachel spills water on the floor. Then, "I'm thirsty. I need some juice," declares Brian. And by the time all needs are met, bedtime has arrived.

"We'll have to try again tomorrow," I tell my husband, as he crawls into his side of the bed.

Evening two: The phone rings incessantly and the dog runs away.

Evening three: I have a baby shower.

Evening four: There's an important business meeting at church we must attend. Well, maybe tomorrow.

Evening five: The lawn must be mowed before the neighbors ask if our mower is broken. By the time my husband comes in, I'm on the phone with a long-distance call.

Evening six: Ah, quality time at last. No meetings, no phone calls, no chores. The kids are in bed. Trivialities emerge. The dog wet the carpet again; the phone bill came; Daniel drew a picture of a dog, and Brian drew a dinosaur; Lew's office was painted the wrong color; his barber retired. Time's up. Here was our quality time, but where were the feelings, the profound discussions, the good times I had envisioned? "Well, we're just out of practice," says my husband. True, but even if we had our regular thirty minutes each evening you cannot schedule profound thoughts or know when ideas will pop into your head or when feelings will be strongest and call to be shared.

Just as our hectic, busy lives shrink the quantity of time we have with our spouses and can make planned quality time awkward, so our quantity/quality time with children suffers—except children have little control over the matter.

A picnic in the park, a trip to the zoo, a day at a museum, hot chocolate and cookies in front of the fireplace: these special times are deliberate and planned—and meaningful. But we can't rely solely upon the special planned events. How could we ever plan or predict when needs will arise or when teachable moments will exist? The more quantity time we spend with our children, the more likely we are to be in the right place at the right time. We'll have more opportunities to hug them, to tell them we love them, to share God's love with them, and to tell them how wonderful they are.

Quantity alone won't guarantee quality, but each family must decide what quantity is right for them to meet their children's needs and to fit their situation. The time must continually be reassessed and monitored to be sure the goals are being met. And the family must make sure the quality is there, too.

If we're to heed the command in Deuteronomy, we must be with our children to teach them. As we are with them through the ins and outs of daily living, we can seize their teachable moments. We can speak of the beauty of God's creation as we plant periwinkle in the yard. We can talk of the value of family as we dust the family pictures. We can sing old favorites such as "Jesus Loves Me" as we travel in the car. We can teach them the value of laughter as we laugh at our own mistakes and at the little pitfalls that dot our paths.

As you are at home and as you are away, as you rest and as you work, may your children know of your love and may they know of God's love. ॐ

51

⇻ 16 ⇺
Do As I Do

Since you are God's dear children, you must try to be like him. Your life must be controlled by love, just as Christ loved us and gave his life for us as a sweet-smelling offering and sacrifice that pleases God.

—Ephesians 5:1–2 (GNB)

> *Do as I do,*
> *And do as I say,*
> *For what I do say,*
> *Is what I do do.*
> ⇻ ⇺

My sons were given a questionnaire for their "Me" book in preschool. They dictated their answers to the teachers. For the question "What do you want to be when you grow up?" both of the boys answered, "Daddy." What an awesome responsibility for my husband! Two little shadows, following him around, wanting to be like him when they grow up!

And this is common for all of us, fathers and mothers. Our children are watching us, taking in what we do and what we say. To them, this is the way it is, and the way it should be. They don't innately know better if what we do is wrong. Much of what they see us do will become natural to them, second nature to them in their own actions and speech. One of the greatest gifts that we can give them is a good example to live by: good actions, attitudes, and speech.

The little ditty above is what we as Christian parents need to be able to say to our children, not the old saying, "Do as I say and not as I do." We need to be examples our children can follow.

What do you want your children to be like when they grow up? The standards you set for their future may be higher than those you set for yourself. Now ask yourself, Would I be willing to have my children grow up and be like me? I'm not talking here about personality traits that really don't matter—whether they're extremely organized or more spontaneous, whether they're the life of the party or would prefer a quiet evening with a few friends, and so forth. I am talking about values, morals, fruits of the Spirit that are very important. Are you living a life that you would be pleased to have your children emulate when they grow up?

I realized recently an area of weakness that I have and that I am in danger of passing on to my own children: the development and nurturing of friendships. I value friendships, but I don't allow them to claim the priority that they should in my life. I want to have close friends, but I'm not very good at giving of myself to develop a friendship. I will complain that I don't have close friendships like I used to in college, but I fail to initiate calls or activities with those friends that I do have.

As a result, I don't give my children opportunities to be playing with other children here at our house or at friends' houses. I don't model for them what a friend should be. I fail to show them that friendship takes risk at times, that friendship is not always easy but is worth the effort, that friendship is an important part of life. And so, they risk having the same trouble in twenty-five years that I am having now.

So I've taken the first step: realizing the problem. But I'm good at that. I analyze myself over and over. But now comes the hard part: doing something about it so that my children can have a model of friendship.

And that, of course, is only one of my weaknesses. What about yours? Is it something you don't do that you should do, like mine, or is it something you do that you shouldn't do?

One essential area that we should model for our children is marriage. From where else will a child's primary model of marriage come? How will your children believe that a marriage partner is to be treated—with respect, love, honor, and forgiveness, or with disrespect, ridicule, bitterness, and scorn? Will your children believe that marriage is "for better or for worse," or "till debt and problems and boredom do us part"?

When I realized that my sons would probably look (unconsciously, of course) for a wife that is a lot like dear old Mom, I really started to straighten up. I want the best wives possible for my sons, and I'm sure that few of the girls they date will be good enough for my little boys (my mother-in-law claims that most of the girls my husband and his brother dated were real "bimbos"), so I knew I had to be as wonderful as possible to get their standards set as high as possible. (I think I am fairly wonderful in their eyes at present, but I'm sure I will have slipped in the ratings by the time they become teenagers.) If for any reason it is not possible for you to model in the marriage arena now, think of the other aspects of male/female relationships that you can model for your children: respectful dating, friendships, honesty, contentment, forgiveness, and more.

Most of us, however, fail to be perfect examples at all times. This gives us the opportunity to set for our children one of the very best examples—the example of a person who truly knows how to say "I'm sorry." I make my children say those words many times in the course of a day. They certainly don't like to say the words, and it's only because I'm standing over them with threats in my eyes that they mutter a muffled "Sorry." Sincerity is not always present with the words. But that's where I can model for them.

Because I fail to live up to all the standards that I set, I have many opportunities to model a sincere and humble "I'm sorry." I get angry and bite off their heads. I forget to keep a promise. I get angry and bite off their heads. I get too busy in my own preoccupations to listen to their needs. I get angry and bite off their heads. And I say, "I'm sorry." And they learn that I'm not perfect, and they don't have to expect themselves to be perfect, either. And they learn how to admit their mistakes and shortcomings—an important element in human relationships, and in their pathway to a personal relationship to God.

Most importantly, though, we can model the trip along that pathway to a personal relationship with God. We are admittedly imperfect examples. How many times do we hear words from our children's lips or see reactions or expressions or attitudes that shouldn't be there, only to realize that they learned those unpleasantries from us?

We will be their primary models, be assured. We can do our best to be able to instruct, as Paul did, "Imitate me, then, just as I imitate Christ" (1 Corinthians 11:1, GNB). But if we can steer our children primarily to the flawless example of Jesus Christ, then their eyes can be fixed on him instead. ࿏

⇛ 17 ⇚
Preschool Mutant Ninja Turtles

*Do not be conformed to this world but be transformed by the
renewal of your mind, that you may prove what is the will of God,
what is good and acceptable and perfect.*

—*Romans 12:2 (RSV)*

⇛ ⇚

My boys made it through four and a half years without develop-
ing any "sock-'em-up" hero worship of characters from TV. They
had admired the Sesame Street characters, but Big Bird and Ernie
and Snuffy and Elmo were OK because they taught about letters
and numbers, about friendship and following rules; and they gave
my children multi-ethnic exposure that they didn't get in our
W.A.S.P. neighborhood. Even Oscar the Grouch I could put up
with.

Later, Brian and Daniel were drawn to the Disney characters.
Mickey Mouse and friends are basically wholesome, so I had no
trouble with that.

Soon, of course, dinosaurs became a consuming passion. That
was great, because I saw that as an opportunity to build my sons'
appreciation of science and learning.

When Batman fever hit the country, my nostalgic husband went
around the house singing, "DA-da-DA-da-DA-da-DA-da, DA-da-
DA-da-DA-da-DA-da, BATMAN!" It barely fazed my boys.

But then, here and there, other boys began little by little exposing my boys to the Teenage Mutant Ninja Turtles. I heard intermit-
tent rumblings of turtles now and again, and those rumbles would
fade away as they had come. Suddenly, like a volcanic explosion
that had been spurting off little warning clouds, the infatuation
erupted full-force.

My little boys' conversations became peppered with the names
"Leonardo," "Michelangelo," "Raphael," and "Donatello." No, I
was not exposing them to art appreciation courses. My preschoolers were learning the names of the four mutant turtles who lived
in the sewer, ate pepperoni-and-peanut-butter pizza, and prac-
ticed the art of Ninja fighting to ward off the schemes of the evil
Shredder ("a kitchen utensil?" Raphael asked).

Since I first heard the doctor say, "It's a boy! It's another boy!" I knew this time would be coming, with one gimmick or another. To prepare myself, I had read articles on violent play and violent toys. The main conclusion I reached was that there are as many opinions on the effect and philosophy of toy guns as there are parents, even within the Christian community. The plan I eventually devised was to "allow but not encourage." I planned to monitor their play to keep things under control and to throw in an occasional word on "pretend" and on "good versus evil."

However, I quickly learned that there is much more to this issue than "how will a child's pretending affect his reality?"

As background, you must realize the history of my sons' social interactions. They are basically introverts. I can relate to that and I can encourage the individuality that each of them has, but I also realize that they need basic social skills to relate to others. I know that they need to feel comfortable with themselves in order to maintain positive self-esteem. Neither of my sons had been strong in the social skills area. Even at my prompting, they would rarely say hello or good-bye to strangers, acquaintances, or friends.

Meanwhile, back at the ranch . . . Daniel and Brian had both been admiring Teenage Mutant Ninja Turtle watches in a catalog. Lewwy and I decided to use their desire for these to teach them a bit about earning and saving money, so we had them save their meager allowance and do some extra work in the house. When the boys had earned sufficient money, we ordered a Leonardo watch and a Donatello watch.

The big day came. The watches arrived in the mail, and my four-year-old boys were transformed into Preschool Mutant Ninja Turtles. My little introverts were walking up to strangers in the doctor's office, strangers in the drugstore, and strangers at the ball field, and saying, "Look, Mister, I've got a Teenage Mutant Ninja Turtle watch. His name is Leonardo, he's blue, the numbers on the watch say 3 and 4 and 5, and my mother's measurements are. . . ." (Well, not quite all of that.)

I also saw that now my boys had an immediate common ground with every other little boy they came upon. As soon as Brian or Daniel would meet another boy, they would all begin talking or playing Ninja Turtles. This was the same Brian and Daniel who had kept mostly to themselves throughout the four years of their lives. Their social life had improved 200 percent.

Teenage Mutant Ninja Turtles had brought them out of their shells.

These "heroes in a half shell" had assaulted me with a difficult issue of parenting: How much of your values do you **force** your children to live by? I'm not talking about avoiding promiscuity, stealing, lying, murdering, and other blatant sins, but about the more subtle and complex values. When a child's self-esteem is so essential and yet so vulnerable, do we have the right to say, for example, "No, you will not have any of the popular toys that your peers have because I don't believe in violence." Or, "No, you will not have the nice clothes that your friends have because I don't believe in materialism." We have the right to expect ourselves to live by those standards, but how tightly do we hold our children to our standards?

Being a Christian is not always an easy job: being different, having integrity in a world of compromise, loving the "unlovely" in plain view of the "beautiful people," giving money to our church instead of keeping up with the Joneses—being "transformed" rather than "conformed to this world."

I try to live by that Scripture in my Christian walk. I resist being "conformed to this world"—but I am an adult, with an established self-esteem, who realizes that doing what is right in God's sight is more important than doing what others approve of. I have made Christ my Savior and Lord, and so I have his Holy Spirit to transform me "by the renewal of my mind." But should I expect my children, with their fragile and growing self-esteem, to live as I do? *Can* I expect my children, who are not yet old enough to call upon the Holy Spirit for power, to submit to the same standards that I hold for myself?

Should I? Can I? Should you? Can you?

I don't think I can insist that my children answer to all the same standards that I answer to myself, though I can model those standards and encourage my children to reach for them, too. What I must determine, with the Lord's help, is where to draw the line for Rachel and Daniel and Brian.

Where will you draw your line? ૐ

⋙ Part V ⋘

Old Mother Pidge: The Stages of Childhood

Old Mother Pidge
  Leaned over the fridge
To fetch her young baby a bottle.
  But when she stood up
  He was holding a cup
And so had no need for that bottle.

She went for a walker
  So he'd roam around,
But when she got home
  He could run 'cross the ground.

She bought him a game
  That would teach him to count,
He grabbed checkbook and pen and asked,
  "What was that amount?"

She bought him a tape
  Of Mother Goose rhymes;
He just shook his head saying,
  "Mom, get with the times."
She checked out some books
  On the birds and the bees;
He handed them back and said,
  "I don't need these."

She put down some tissues,
  On the pew, in a pile,
As her baby and his new wife
  Marched down the aisle. ॐ

⇛ 18 ⇚

Hope

To have faith is to be sure of the things we hope for, to be certain of the things we cannot see.

—*Hebrews 11:1 (GNB)*

⇛ ⇚

Have you ever envied your friends or relatives who don't have kids yet? Though you love your kids and wouldn't take them back for a refund, do you sometimes look with longing upon the life-styles of those couples who haven't yet reached the parenting stage?

Life for them is relatively simple. They stay out late if they want, and have only themselves to prepare for bed. They eat dinner at nice restaurants, and when they eat out, they cut only their own food. They peacefully enjoy the conversation and savor the meal, and are blissfully unaware (or would be if they knew the alternative) of the effect their presence is having on the other diners. They almost always sleep through the night; but should they fall behind on their sleep, it's only a matter of time till they find the opportunity to catch up. They don't have to consider the cost and effort of getting a babysitter as they contemplate an evening out. And when they do have an evening out, it's based in large part upon where they themselves want to go.

Yet rarely do these unencumbered souls appreciate the ease of their lot. The desire to procreate must certainly be a God-given desire, for why else would sane persons trade that life for one in which they take twice as long to get ready to go somewhere, have only half as many possible places to go, half as much money to use, half as much time to spend, and will be called upon to use more than twice the amount of patience they are accustomed to doling out.

I confess that I was very unappreciative of my b.c. (before children) lifestyle. My maternal urgings were strong, and I longed to add another member to our household. While my urges were still unfulfilled, I *knew* things would be better when I had a baby.

I became pregnant and ecstatic. I was told I was carrying twins and was undaunted. Then I delivered. I brought the babies home—I was terrified of the first day that I was to go solo. It was a lot of work, but I *knew* things would get easier.

And things do get easier. A baby smiles and starts giving back. She realizes what toys are for and can amuse herself for longer periods. She eats finger foods, uses a cup and spoon. She learns to communicate and tell you what she wants.

Yet I have heard my pastor (father of four grown children) say that parenting does not get easier—it gets different and more difficult. But I just cannot bring myself to believe him. True, there is a flip side to everything: the toddler who can now walk by himself to the car can also run across a parking lot; the preschooler who no longer needs diapers often hears Mother Nature calling at the most inopportune times and places. I also realize that the potential sources of conflict are much more serious as a child grows older: drugs instead of candy, arguments over dating instead of demands to go to the playground, teen pregnancy instead of innocent games of "doctor," and car accidents instead of scraped knees.

The difficulty of the early days lies not in the magnitude of the demands, but their constancy: the constant physical and emotional demands of the infant/toddler/preschool years, leaving little time for rejuvenation and recovery. Preschool motherhood, especially with more than one preschooler around, is not a matter of "one thing after another"; it's "one thing and another at the very same time." Yes, my pastor has been through all the stages, and I have not. Yet, isn't it possible that his memory has purified its pictures of the past?

I like the way the writer of Ecclesiastes warns us about yearning for the good old days: "Never ask, 'Oh, why were things so much better in the old days?' It's not an intelligent question" (Ecclesiastes 7:10, GNB). The only parent I unguardedly believe when comparing stages is the one who currently has a child at each stage being compared—but even those comparisons are colored by the personalities of the children involved.

I remember that I did begin to feel calmer and more in control when my sons were reaching the end of toddlerhood. Well, then Rachel came along and the lull was over; but when she, too, reached that stage, I was again renewed. They did get easier, but I also had gotten wiser and more accomplished.

Regardless, though, of whether I am correct or my pastor is

correct, I know that my sanity demands that I believe in my point of view. Knowing how trying these early years can be, how would I survive if I knew it was only to get harder? I need that hope to hang on to. Perhaps one of the reasons that God doesn't allow us to see into the future is that we would tend to focus on the trials to come instead of hoping for the good and having faith in the divine presence in the future.

I have hopes that in the days to come my job as a mother will in many ways get easier. Yet because the future is so unknown, that hope alone won't do. My faith is the strength that keeps me moving ahead—a faith that whatever happens, Christ will help me through, that if my eyes are on him now, he will use the difficulties I face to strengthen me and help me grow, to be better able to face the challenges of elementary motherhood, of adolescent motherhood, and of adult motherhood. ❧

⇥≫ 19 ≪⇤

The Grass Is Always Greener

I know what it is to be in need and what it is to have more than enough. I have learned this secret, so that anywhere, at any time, I am content . . . .

—Philippians 4:12 (GNB)

⇥≫ ≪⇤

Picture the poster of four cows, each in separate fields that converge like a four-square game. Each cow is convinced that her neighbor's grass is greener and tastier, so each cow is straining through the fence towards her neighbor's pasture while the cow in that pasture is straining towards the next cow's pasture—and so on.

Now picture the single girl saying, "Ah, when I'm married—then I'll be complete!" And the young married woman saying, "If only I could have a baby!" And the mother of an infant saying, "I can't wait till my baby can walk!" And the mother of a toddler, "When will this child ever be potty trained?" The preschool mother, "Just imagine all the time I'll have when Junior can totally dress himself—and when he goes to school!" And the elementary mother, "I'm a taxicab driver with no meter and no tips! Oh, but when my daughter gets her license . . . !" The adolescent mother, "When, oh when, will my child start acting like a human being again?" And the parent of grown children, "Oh, for the good old days!"

I have yet to pass through the last three pastures, but I must confess I've truly acted the part of the cow on four of the first five—waiting for the future, straining for the grass on the other side of the fence. I have been so guilty of the grass-is-greener syndrome that I even caught myself admiring the grass in pastures I had left—and that was when I saw the folly of my ways.

During one of motherhood's more rocky times, I found myself looking with a bit of envy at the relatively unharnessed lifestyle of friends without children. I thought, "Now why didn't I appreciate that freedom when it was mine?" Then it hit me, like a farmer's stick on my rump, as I was moo-ved to realize, "No, I didn't really appreciate the green grass of life without children. Nor am I

64

appreciating the special vegetation of life with preschoolers. And if I keep up at this pace, I will be so busy looking at the pastures to come and those that have gone that I will miss the clover, the apple trees, and all the other specialties that each pasture holds." I knew then that as a mother, I needed to start milking each phase for all it was worth, before it was too late: the cuddling of infancy, such close, intimate, peaceful togetherness, a baby asleep in your arms; the eagerness of toddlerhood, learning to run, to climb, to play, to test her wings, to talk more and more and more, to smell the roses; the pretend worlds of preschoolers, where mom and dad are still welcome participants and laughter is still unrestrained.

I'm not saying that hope and anticipation are not soothing and even necessary, but all Christians should learn, as the apostle Paul did, to be content in all situations (Philippians 4:12).

As a content Christian, or a satisfied cow (I found this analogy particularly easy to relate to while I was nursing my babies), you can look for the specialties of each stage of your child's growth. As you look around your pasture, find the shimmering dewdrops, the brightly colored flowers and the soft, pastel flowers, the deep, comforting grasses, and the rocks to climb and play on—and resolve to romp and play and rest with your very special child in the grasses of this very pasture—while there's still time. ❧

→≫ Part VI ≪←
There Was a Little Woman: A Mother's Noble Profession

There was a little woman,
  As I have heard tell,
She went to market
  Her eggs for to sell,
She went to market
  All on a market day,
And she fell asleep
  On the King's highway.

There came by a pedlar
  His name was Stout,
He cut her petticoats
  All round about;
He cut her petticoats
  Up to her knees,
Which made the poor woman
  To shiver and sneeze.

When the little woman
　　Began to awake
She began to shiver,
　　And she began to shake;
She began to shake,
　　And she began to cry,
Goodness mercy on me,
　　This is none of I!

If it be not I,
　　As I suppose it be,
I have a little dog at home,
　　And he know me;
If it be I,
　　He'll wag his little tail,
And if it be not I,
　　He'll loudly bark and wail.

Home went the little woman,
　　All in the dark,
Up jumped the little dog,
　　And he began to bark.
He began to bark,
　　And she began to cry,
Goodness mercy on me,
　　I see I be not I!

This poor little woman
　　Passed the night on a stile,
She shivered with cold,
　　And she trembled the while;
She slept not a wink
　　But was all night awake,
And was heartily glad
　　When morning did break.

There came by the pedlar
   Returning from town,
She asked him for something
   To match her short gown,
The sly pedlar rogue
   Showed the piece he purloined,
Said he to the woman,
   It will do nicely joined.

She pinned on the piece,
   And exclaimed, What a match!
I am lucky indeed
   Such a bargain to catch.
The dog wagged his tail,
   And she began to cry,
Goodness mercy on me,
   I've discovered it be I![17]

Marsh's moral for mothers:
Don't let a roguish society convince you
that you be not you. ð

➽ 20 ⠦

"Do You Work?"

"The righteous will then answer him, 'When, Lord, did we ever see you hungry and feed you, or thirsty and give you a drink? When did we ever see you a stranger and welcome you in our homes, or naked and clothe you? When did we ever see you sick or in prison, and visit you?' The King will reply, 'I tell you, whenever you did this for one of the least important of these brothers of mine, you did it for me!'"

—Matthew 25:37–40 (GNB)

➽ ⠦

I had grasped one of my children's "teachable moments" one day to have a minilesson on careers. We talked a little bit about what Daddy did, what Uncle David did, what Aunt Susie did, and so forth. And then, fishing for a little affirmation for myself on my blooming career as a writer, I asked them, "And what is Mommy's job?"

"Your job is taking care of us, Mommy," Daniel answered.

I looked up at him (for at that moment I felt low enough to look up at the tips of the pile on our carpet) and smiled. "Yes, Daniel, you're right. That is the most important job that I have."

Why is it often hard for those of us who are at-home mothers to truly recognize the importance of what we do? Why is it often hard for outsiders to recognize our position as a legitimate and essential job?

When I first became an at-home mother and had no "employment" at all, I could never bring myself to give a straight answer to the clerks who were giving my checks the once-over.

"Home phone number?" they would ask.

That was easy enough to answer.

"Office number?"

Gulp. "Same."

I could never bring myself to answer "None." Here I was performing one of the most important—and sometimes one of the most difficult—duties on the face of the earth, and I felt insignificant.

I've never been one to be overly concerned about what others think, but in my "previous life"—as a student and then as an employee—my concept of myself was always very focused on my achievements and accomplishments, my mastery of the subject matter and my performance of my duties. Besides the facts that I had conceived and carried my children and they were still alive, what other accomplishments were apparent in my job? I certainly did not feel I had any mastery of my subject matter, and I often felt inadequate in my job performance.

Fate, however, does not always let me get away with my little charades of looking for importance elsewhere. I recently went to a local university law library to do some research for my writing. As I was standing in the elevator, I became embarrassingly aware that the back of the legal pad I was carrying was covered with preschool scribbles. Discreetly, I turned the pad around, so that the page covered with important-looking adult notes was showing. I soon became aware that the preschool scribbles had been scribbled in colored chalk. Turning the scribbles away from public view had exposed them to the front of my white shirt. I got what I deserved.

A friend of mine offers added proof that being an at-home mother is a difficult job. Winnie had her training and experience as a nuclear engineer. Hers was a job that took a great deal of mental prowess and that was filled with pressures and stresses and conflicts. She continued her job after her children were born, but later, when the kids were three and five, she decided that she needed to quit her job and devote her energy to her children, regardless of the resulting financial sacrifice.

Soon after her job switch, I heard her say something that I love to ask her to repeat from time to time: "Being a full-time nuclear engineer was a whole lot easier than being at home with my kids all the time!"

Staying at home with your children full-time may involve many stresses. One of the largest problems that I encounter is isolation and lack of a support system. Throughout the growing-up years, friendships come rather naturally. You meet your friends at school, at church, or in your neighborhood and have lots of opportunities to be with them and build friendships. College friendships can be even more wonderful because you share so many aspects of daily life. Then during the years of employment, you have the interaction with other employees and perhaps clients, patients, students, or customers.

And then comes motherhood, where you could conceivably stay in your house all day long, seven days a week, and see no one except the UPS delivery man or the postman ringing for postage due. You may make it out to the grocery store, but while you're there you're too busy calming a fussing child or attempting to halter a wild one to appreciate the adult contact.

Another mother of twins explained her system: "I stay at home till I'm going crazy seeing the same four walls. Then I take the kids out and it's such a hassle that I swear I'll never leave the house again. Then I stay at home till I'm going crazy seeing the same four walls. Then. . . ."

Which brings me to another difficulty of being at home full-time. In my b.c. days, I was rarely home. I didn't care if the house was messy or needed this piece of furniture or this room painted. But now I see the house's flaws all day long and am constantly reminded of what I'm not getting done. And if you're like me, you're too embarrassed by your ever-messy, ever-dirty, poorly-decorated-from-lack-of-money house to invite many people over.

There's more. The at-home mother's job often involves constant and persistent demands, demands made by children who are often whining, fussing, or crying as they seek to get what they want, taxing mom's patience and raising her blood pressure. If there are two or more children in the home, there will be squabbles and fights for mom to intervene in, referee, judge, and terminate. If there is only one child, he or she may be demanding more of mom's attention as playmate or companion. If the children no longer take naps, or if they take their naps at different times, mom may have no break, no time to call her own.

Each day may bear a frustrating sameness to the day before, and the nine-to-five slot will be quite similar to the activities and demands before and after that usual workday time period.

This weary mother may be frustrated by a lack of outside stimulation—little time for hobbies, for reading, for exercise, for simply playing and relaxing. She may feel stifled by a new lack of spontaneity, for she can no longer just pick up and go. She must either find a babysitter, or she must get the kids dressed and shoed and bundled, out the door to the car, in the car seats with the seatbelts on, and then wonder how they'll do once they get there.

This mother, who may already be struggling with depression, may have to use her utmost self-discipline in handling the tight family budget. The fact that she has no employment may severely limit her spending habits. Her lunches, in fact, may be a tired procession of peanut butter sandwiches, tuna fish, and canned soups. Dinners similarly may be stuck in a rut of what she knows the kids will usually eat: spaghetti, pizza, frozen chicken nuggets, fish sticks, hot dogs, and sloppy joes. Each of those tedious meals comes too often: mom feels as if she has no sooner cleaned up from one meal than the next meal is begging to be fixed.

At-home mom spends most of her waking hours being totally unselfish, but then she feels guilty when she begins thinking selfish thoughts.

And for all of these strains in her job, she has few tangible perks. She may see few accomplishments to point to and say, "Hey! Look what I've done!" The house gets cluttered and dirty more quickly than it gets straightened and cleaned, and she sees no absolute proof that her children are doing better than they would have at a babysitter's house. She gets no weekly paycheck, no health insurance or sick days, no Christmas bonus, no merit raises.

And then someone has the nerve to ask, "Do you work?"

There are indeed good days, and there are good moments. But there are many days when the good flickers only like a dying ember in an oppressive darkness.

No, if you are an at-home mom you probably do not often get the affirmation you deserve for the important job you are doing. But remember what Jesus said: " 'Whenever you did this for one of the least important of these brothers of mine, you did it for me!' " (Matthew 25:40, GNB). He also said, "Let the children come to me and do not stop them, because the Kingdom of heaven belongs to such as these" (Matthew 19:14, GNB). Although the world may fail to truly recognize their importance, these children that God has given you to raise are *very* important.

And God gives us this promise:

"My grace is sufficient for you, for my power is made perfect in weakness." (And then Paul added) I will all the more gladly boast of my weaknesses, that the power of Christ may rest upon me. For the sake of Christ, then, I am content with weaknesses, insults, hardships, persecutions, and calamities; for when I am weak, then I am strong *(2 Corinthians 12:9–10, RSV).*

Yes, I sure have had a lot of "strong" days here recently. ৯৶

→»» 21 «««←
Loving Your Job

Whatever you do, work at it with all your heart, as though you were working for the Lord and not for men. Remember that the Lord will give you as a reward what he has kept for his people. For Christ is the real Master you serve.

—Colossians 3:23–24 (GNB)

→»» «««←

If you decided to carry a lantern and set off in search of an employee who obviously dislikes his or her job, you would probably find the assignment to be sadly simple. The grumpy sales clerk, the unsmiling nurse, the gruff dentist, the sarcastic waitress—all are too easy to find each day.

These people are living out one of my pet peeves: people who grumble about their jobs. If they can change jobs, then they should change. If they can't change, they should make the most of the situation.

I used to get a certain sense of self-satisfaction at observing grumbling employees, wishing I had the nerve to lecture them on job satisfaction. When I stepped off my mental soapbox, I returned promptly to my own thoughts: "It's only two-thirty. Three more hours till Lewwy gets home to help me with the kids. (sigh) How many more years until they go to school? I never have any time to myself."

And then I caught myself in my hypocrisy. I was not about to quit my job, though, so I knew I had better make the most of it.

Although mothers receive no financial compensation for their work, and the government certainly doesn't offer us many tax breaks for staying home with our children, motherhood is, nevertheless, a job, and can even be called a vocation. Both of *The American Heritage Dictionary*'s definitions of "vocation" can be appropriate: "1. A regular occupation or profession; especially, one for which one is specially suited or qualified."[18] (Although I don't always feel qualified for the tasks of motherhood, I know that no one is more suited than I am: who loves my children more than I do? Who desires the best for them more than I?) "2. An urge or predisposition to undertake a certain kind of work, especially a religious career; a calling."[19] I feel certain that this job is where God wants me right now, that the "food" I am working for (John 6:27) is the souls and well-being of my children.

As a worker, a mother can benefit from the advice of a book like Stanley Baldwin's *Take This Job and Love It.* One chapter that captured my attention was "Making a Boring Job Interesting." Although "boring" is not an adjective I use much to describe my job, "lack of intellectual stimulation or challenge" does often apply. One of Baldwin's suggestions in that chapter can especially be applied to mothering. He recommends "job enrichment"— finding "interesting elements" in our jobs that we may not have recognized before.[20]

I happened upon a toll booth operator the other day who had somehow anticipated my need for a receipt. I hadn't even gotten the words, "Receipt, please," out of my mouth when he had handed the slip of paper to me. He grinned when he saw the surprise on my face. I wondered as I drove away if that was his method of making a very tedious job into something amusing.

Even preschool mothers have "job enrichment" possibilities. Here are a few that I've dreamed up:

1. Become an expert on children's literature, trying out all the appropriate award-winning books on your own children. Christian publishers offer an excellent selection of books (as well as videos and tapes) for children of all ages.

2. Invent creative meals—cookie cutter sandwiches, monster-face muffins, and so forth. Just don't expect your little gourmets to be always grateful!

3. Familiarize yourself with your children's favorite TV show and write a story with those characters and your children. Imagine Big Bird and Snuffy coming to visit at your house!

4. Provide arts and crafts opportunities, especially those you can enjoy together. For example, use sponges cut into shapes and dipped into paint to decorate your own wrapping paper. Use some of the finished products as gifts—to relatives or to an elderly acquaintance or to someone you know who is sick.

5. Reacquaint yourself with your own childhood favorites: watch with your children *Bambi, The Littlest Angel,* the holiday Charlie Brown specials; read together Dr. Seuss, *Charlotte's Web,* or other books from your childhood library.

6. If you like being outside, move much of your life out there. You may even shift emphasis from decorating your house to decorating your yard. Though neither an immaculate house nor a showplace yard is achievable or even desirable now, the fresh air and a measure of productivity will be therapeutic for mother and child. This strategy will also give your child less opportunity to mess up the house!

One of my own "interesting elements" has been pretend play. The ham in me has re-emerged. Though Rich Little has no need to fear competition from me, I have enjoyed imitating characters such as Ernie and Bert, Oscar the Grouch, Goofy and Minnie Mouse, Ducky, and all the animals on the ark. I did, however, wonder if I'd carried my element too far when I picked my twenty-one-month-old up from the church nursery only to have the sitter say, "I knew she was your little girl when I asked her what a duck said and she did a mallard imitation instead of saying 'quack-quack'!" ࿇

⇢≫ 22 ≪⇠

Job Stress

*. . . Consider yourselves fortunate when all kinds of trials come
your way, for you know that when your faith succeeds in facing
such trials, the result is the ability to endure.*

—*James 1:2–3 (GNB)*

⇢≫ ≪⇠

The Preschool Mother Stress Test

Answer the following questions, giving yourself the appropriate
points as suggested, to determine your preschool mother stress
level.

_____ 1. How many children do you have? Give yourself points
as follows:
—5 points for a newborn
—4 points for an infant
—3 points for a toddler
—2 points for a preschooler
—1 point for an elementary school child
—5 points for a preteen or teenager in the throes of
puberty or adolescence
—3 additional points for twins
—5 additional points for triplets or larger multiples

_____ 2. How many times per night are you generally awakened
by a needy child? Give yourself 1 point for each distur-
bance.

_____ 3. Do your children still nap? If so, deduct 1 point for each
nap per child. If not, give yourself 2 points.

_____ 4. How many times do you have to get up from the table
during a typical meal? Give yourself 1 point per trip to
the sink, refrigerator, paper towel roll, and so forth.

_____ 5. Are any of your children going through a particularly rough stage (such as the terrible two's)? If so, give yourself 1 point per child in transition. (If it's a really bad stage, throw in some extra points!)

_____ 6. Rank each child's personality in terms of difficulty or easygoingness, on a scale of 1–3, 1 being easygoing and 3 being fussy or demanding. Give yourself points accordingly. (Example: your four-year-old is a dream child and your eighteen-month-old is a holy terror, you get 4 points (1 + 3).) Do not, however, reveal the results to your children if they fall near the difficult end of the scale!

_____ 7. Rank your husband's helpfulness around the house and with the children on a scale of 1–5, 1 being the most helpful, 5 the least. Give yourself points accordingly: if your husband is ideal, you get 1 point, but if he's no help, you get 5. If you're a single mom, give yourself 10 points!

_____ 8. How much help do you get from outside sources— regular babysitter, mother's helper, cleaning lady, other family members, and so forth? Deduct 1 point per hour of help you get in the average week.

_____ 9. How many children do you generally take with you to the grocery store? Give yourself 1 point per child.

_____10. Rank your present relationship with your husband on a scale of 0–10, 0 being the best. To give yourself stress points accordingly, subtract 5 from your rank. For example, a superb relationship, with a ranking of 0, gives you a −5 (your marriage actually helps your stress level). A struggling marriage, with a ranking of 10, gives you 5 stress points.

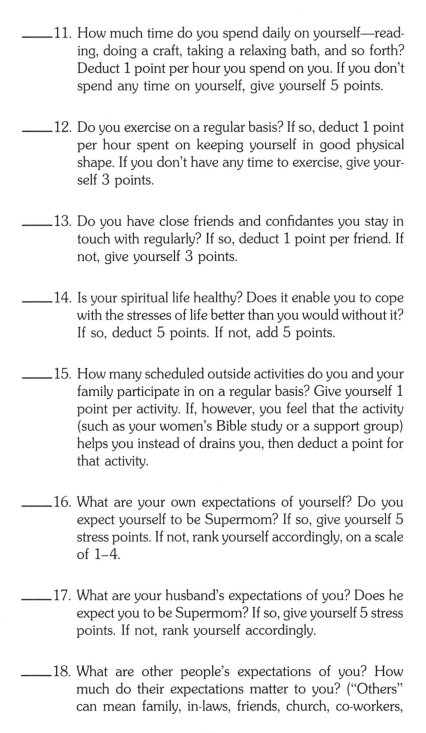

_____11. How much time do you spend daily on yourself—reading, doing a craft, taking a relaxing bath, and so forth? Deduct 1 point per hour you spend on you. If you don't spend any time on yourself, give yourself 5 points.

_____12. Do you exercise on a regular basis? If so, deduct 1 point per hour spent on keeping yourself in good physical shape. If you don't have any time to exercise, give yourself 3 points.

_____13. Do you have close friends and confidantes you stay in touch with regularly? If so, deduct 1 point per friend. If not, give yourself 3 points.

_____14. Is your spiritual life healthy? Does it enable you to cope with the stresses of life better than you would without it? If so, deduct 5 points. If not, add 5 points.

_____15. How many scheduled outside activities do you and your family participate in on a regular basis? Give yourself 1 point per activity. If, however, you feel that the activity (such as your women's Bible study or a support group) helps you instead of drains you, then deduct a point for that activity.

_____16. What are your own expectations of yourself? Do you expect yourself to be Supermom? If so, give yourself 5 stress points. If not, rank yourself accordingly, on a scale of 1–4.

_____17. What are your husband's expectations of you? Does he expect you to be Supermom? If so, give yourself 5 stress points. If not, rank yourself accordingly.

_____18. What are other people's expectations of you? How much do their expectations matter to you? ("Others" can mean family, in-laws, friends, church, co-workers, and so forth.) Rank yourself on a scale of 1–5 accordingly. For example, if others expect a lot of you, and that really matters to you, then give yourself a 5.

_____19. What "new" situations are present in your household? (new community, new job, new baby, new marriage, new house, and so forth) Give yourself 5 points for each "new," even if it's a good "new."

_____20. What other difficulties are you having in your life now? (financial problems, marital problems, illness, death of a family member or close friend, and so forth) Give yourself the points you think you deserve, remembering that 1 is low stress and 20 is very high.

For Employed Mothers Only

_____21. Do you enjoy your job? If not, give yourself 1 point.

_____22. Is your job a high-pressure, high-stress job? If so, give yourself stress points (1–3) accordingly.

_____23. Are you satisfied with your decision to work outside of the home, or would you rather be home with your children? If you would rather be home, or if you feel guilty because you're not at home, then give yourself stress points (1–3) accordingly.

_____24. Do others (husband, family, friends) make you feel guilty for your decision to work? If so, give yourself 1 point.

_____25. If your children are in any kind of day-care or after-school care situation, are you pleased with their care? If not, give yourself stress points (1–3) according to how displeased you are.

_____26. Is your job adaptable enough that you can also meet your children's needs when they arise (such as sickness and school programs)? If not, give yourself 1 point.

_____27. Are you satisfied that you are able to spend adequate time with your children in your off-work hours? If not, give yourself 2 points.

For at-Home Mothers Only

_____28. Give yourself 5 automatic stress points for the pressure involved in full-time care of preschoolers!

_____29. Do you miss the challenge and stimulation of a good job? If so, give yourself stress points (1–3) accordingly.

_____30. Do you feel as though your brain has turned into a marshmallow? If so, give yourself 1 point.

_____31. Do you have regular adult contact during the day? If not, give yourself 2 points.

_____32. Is living on one income a challenge and frustration and strain? Give yourself stress points (1–3) accordingly.

For All

_____ 33. Do you feel that there are never enough hours in a day, your house is always a mess, that someone under three feet tall is always making demands on you, that you never have time or money to spend on yourself, and that there's no light at the end of the tunnel? Give yourself all the stress points (1–20) you feel you deserve.

81

Now, figure out your final score, adding where appropriate and subtracting where appropriate. Determine your results from the figures below.

25 points or less:

Congratulations! Either you have a relatively simple life (although I'm sure it doesn't always feel that way), or you have mastered the technique of managing your stress. Now please share your time or wisdom with someone who scored 26 points or more!

26-50 points:

Your life is moderately stressful and/or you need to learn better ways to handle stress. Try cutting back in areas that you can, learning better stress management techniques, and praying for more guidance in this area. There's hope!

51-75 points:

How in the world are you managing to read this book? Perhaps you remembered to take it up with you last time you climbed the wall! Yes, you deserve the sympathy you long for. See the suggestions in the category above; double them, and add the following: enlist any help that you can—cleaning lady, understanding friends or family, pastor, psychologist! Memorize the book *Bonkers: Why Women Get Stressed Out and What They Can Do About It,* by Dr. Kevin Leman! Remember, too, you're not alone!

76 points or more:

If you *ever* feel sorry for yourself, I can understand why! If you get angry at yourself for feeling sorry for yourself, all I can say is, don't be so hard on yourself! You certainly are going through a lot, and a lot of prayer and help from others are definitely in order. Cut back if you can, learn stress management, and sleep with the book *Bonkers* under your pillow!

Disclaimer: *This is a nonprofessional stress test,* designed by an amateur and showing the biases of this preschool mother! If you feel that stress is really getting you down (regardless of how you scored on this test), professional help can be a godsend! ह

→»» 23 ««←
Overcoming Stress

*"Come to me, all you who are weary and burdened, and I will give
you rest. Take my yoke upon you and learn from me, for I am
gentle and humble in heart, and you will find rest for your souls.
For my yoke is easy and my burden is light."*
→»» ««←

—Matthew 11:28–30 (NIV)

I used to think of my mother as a short-tempered person. When
I went away to college, however, and could begin to view the
situation objectively, I understood that her lack of patience resulted from an overabundance of stress.

I can see a lot of my mother in myself, so I know I must guard
my stress level in order to give my children the best "me" I can.
To do this, I've developed my own personal stress guards. Maybe
some of these can help in your life, too.

1. I mustn't overbook! On a recent business trip, my brother,
Chip, was on an air flight that had overbooked—there were more
passengers than there were seats on the plane. The airlines asked
for volunteers who would give up their reservations on this flight
in exchange for a seat on a later flight *and* for a free round-trip
ticket to any place within the continental United States to be used
at any time within the next year. Chip's hand shot up. Another
flight on the same business trip had the same problem and offered
the same deal. Chip's hand shot up again. My brother and his wife
are now debating where and when to use their two free tickets.

Mother Marsh's Airlines doesn't offer the same deal, however.
If I overbook, all that my preschool passengers get is a short-
tempered, irritable, impatient mother. If my schedule is over-
loaded with commitments and deadlines, then my stress level
goes up and my patience with my children goes down. If my
patience and creativity are used up on Sunday school lessons and
Meals on Wheels and church nursery duty and hostessing another
party, then my children get only the dregs.

As the t-shirt states, "Stress is what happens when your mind
says no and your mouth says yes." My family is my most important commitment right now and I must say yes to them and no

to some things I might have said yes to six years ago.

2. I must guard my expectations. I get quite frustrated by unmet expectations, so I do my best to keep them low and manageable. If, for example, I expect that by lunchtime I will be able to wash and hang out two loads of laundry, mop the kitchen floor, vacuum all the carpets, and pave the driveway, then I probably will get frustrated. If, however, I expect that by lunchtime I will be able to wash and hang out one load of laundry and vacuum some of the carpets and be interrupted many times by preschool requests, then I can meet my expectations. I might even be pleasantly surprised by finding time to vacuum all the carpets.

I've also realized I have to guard my expectations during "quality time" outings with the kids. I remember the Saturday I took Brian and Daniel and Rachel to a wildlife refuge in the Washington, D.C. area. I envisioned an idyllic outing with my children, hiking on the nature trail, enjoying the exercise and breathing in the smells of the outdoors, learning of new plants and spotting new birds, and simply enjoying our time together.

Reality didn't even come near the vision. The kids fought constantly and complained about the two-hour ride. When we finally got there, they whined about the snack.

We finally began our hike. Fifty yards into the woods, four-year-old, thirty-five-pound Brian said, "I'm tired! You carry me."

"Brian," I explained gently, "you're too big for me to carry you on a hike."

He cried and sat down and refused to budge.

I spent several minutes coaxing and pleading, but without success. My patience was quickly spent. I crossed my arms and glared at the kids and said, "Okay, do you just want to get in the car and go back home?"

"Yes!" came the unanimous reply.

We survived our quality time only because I hit upon the idea of pretending that we were all Teenage Mutant Ninja Turtles and that the evil Foot Soldiers were hiding behind the trees.

Now I go into outings and the like prepared for complaints and hitches. If they come, I'm ready to handle them without getting my nose bent out of shape. If they don't come, great!

3. I remind myself, "This, too, shall pass!" When my boys first learned to crawl out of their cribs and postpone their nap times, my blood pressure shot up twenty points: "Oh, no! They'll never take naps again! They'll be crawling out of their cribs and fighting nap time until they graduate from high school!" But Brian and Daniel settled back into the routine a week later, when the novelty had worn off.

When my twin toddlers started throwing food on the floor, my blood pressure again shot up twenty points: "My floor will never be the same! How can I keep saying no at mealtime for seventeen more years?"

But I did keep saying no and removing their food, and they soon learned not to throw their food on the floor. It didn't even take seventeen years.

Now when Rachel crawls out of her crib, I can take it in stride. I can deal with her firmly but calmly, all the while assuring myself in complete confidence, "This, too, shall pass." When Rachel throws her food on the floor, I can reprimand her through my clenched teeth and say, "This, too, shall pass."

When I was a child, I would hear adults say, "It's only a stage." I didn't realize that they were reassuring themselves when they made that statement.

4. I try to remember myself. I realize that taking time for "selfish" activities—exercise, hobbies, reading, friends, writing, support groups, and so forth—can rejuvenate me so I can face my mothering responsibilities again.

5. I must keep life with my husband in shape. If I'm brooding over some "wrong" that Lewwy did to me, then my whole outlook and attitude are affected. On the other hand, if our relationship is thriving, I'm renewed by the knowledge that I'm supported by a concerned, loving spouse.

6. I must keep my spiritual life in shape. If I miss taking a walk for many days in a row, my legs begin feeling crampy and uncomfortable. If I miss my spiritual "exercise," my spiritual life and my emotions get crampy and uncomfortable. As in my relationship with my spouse, if I'm secure in my relationship with God, then I'm renewed by the knowledge of God's presence.

I've realized, too, the advantage of keeping my spiritual life and my life as a mother tuned from the same tuning fork. Stanley Baldwin offers suggestions for this in *Take This Job and Love It.* The chapter entitled "Overcoming Work-Related Stress"[21] can be applied in the job of motherhood, for those who have a job outside the home, and for those who don't. Most helpful is his suggestion that we "work to the glory of God."[22]

To work to the glory of God, we can realize that we are obeying God by performing our duties.[23] As mothers, we must recognize that God expects us to love and nurture our children, so in mothering we are being obedient to God. As Colossians 3:24 points out, if we serve the Lord Christ, our work will be rewarded. A mother doesn't often get recognized for all she does. It's nice to know that God sees, and this recognition can ease our stress.

We are also glorifying God as we serve others.[24] Preschool motherhood is certainly a service-related occupation. Your services are unquestionably needed and useful. As Christ said, "Whatever you did for one of the least of these brothers of mine, you did for me" (Matthew 25:40, NIV).

A spirit of gratitude to God can help us to glorify our Lord.[25] Dr. Hans Selye, a leading researcher on stress and its effects, has noted that "Among all the emotions, those that—more than any others—account for the absence or presence of harmful stress (distress) in human relations are the feelings of gratitude and goodwill. . . ."[26] Realize all that you have to be thankful for as a mother, and keep that gratitude at the front of your thoughts.

Finally, we can work to reflect God's excellence in our tasks.[27] Your "good jobs" reflect God's workmanship. Your efforts as a mother can be an offering to God. And when your efforts result in successes, note the successes and appreciate your own hard work.

Your child spontaneously says "Thank you" or "I'm sorry." He or she spills some milk but cleans it up without being asked. Give your child and yourself some credit and a pat on the back. The frustrations and fussings seem to come more frequently than the obvious successes during this preschool time, so grab every success you can.

And pray frequently to God:

Thank you, God,
That I can obey you by raising my children,
That you have asked and allowed me to be here for them,
That I can serve them and help them to grow to their potential.
Thank you that I can perform this mission for you,
That I can work to accomplish this essential task,
And that you can help me to do the best job possible.

Amen ॐ

86

➤➤ 24 ◄◄

A Woman's Place

The wisdom of the prudent is to give
thought to their ways,
but the folly of fools is deception.
—Proverbs 14:8 (NIV)
➤➤ ◄◄

Adolescence is a time of major change and questions. Because of the turmoil of those times, few adults would want to return, and many parents would like to have their own children skip that stage.

Society is experiencing its own adolescence now, an adolescence of the roles women play.

Women's roles, and each individual's perception of them, have been undergoing change, mostly for the better. But it is not only society that must experience the turmoil and questions of its adolescence—women individually are experiencing the stress of adjustment.

Every woman, whether consciously or unconsciously, must determine her "place." Does she belong in the home, in the business world, or in both? My favorite bumper sticker is the one that says, "A woman's place is in the House—and the Senate." I chuckle and cheer when I read that, yet I return home willingly to my full-time domestic duties as a wife and mother. I believe that a woman belongs in the house and the House. But I'm only in the house, and am foregoing the challenges of the House.

Many "experts" are able to tell you just where women really do belong. Christian authorities, especially, often say that a woman belongs home, raising her children, maintaining the home front, and obeying her husband. And we will do well to listen with discernment to authorities, to give ear to what they say and why they say it, and to use them as beacons in choosing our paths.

But even more important than the experts' opinions is each woman's deepest feelings. Do her feelings concur with her practices or do they conflict?

Answer each of the following questions as quickly and honestly as possible, based not on what you think you should believe, but what you really feel.

1. Are women and men equal in general intellectual capabilities?
2. Are women and men equal in job performance potential?
3. Are women and men equal in career advancement potential (society's artificial barriers aside)?
4. Are women and men equal in status in the eyes of God?
5. Do women and men have innate, God-given differences in the roles they must fulfill as parents, and is the mother necessarily the primary caregiver (as opposed to the father)?

A woman's answers will generally fall into one of the following three categories: June Cleaver, Hope Steadman, and Mrs. Mr. Mom.

1. The woman who answers no to the first four questions, believing that men are indeed superior to women, and yes to number five is rather traditional in her beliefs, a little like Beaver Cleaver's mother, June. This woman's place **is** in the home. She believes she belongs there, and if she can fulfill her role there, then she can be satisfied. Her conflict will come if she must work outside the home to such an extent that her God-given duty as wife and mother must suffer.

2. The woman who answers yes to the first four questions (or no because she believes that women are superior!) and yes to question five has a lot in common with "thirtysomething's" Hope Steadman. This woman may have difficulty in knowing or accepting exactly where her place is. This would be the category that would fit most of the women in our society today.

"I have as much potential as a man in the 'outside world,' but I have to sacrifice many years of this potential," says the Hope who has chosen to stay at home to raise her children. She may envy working women who are continuing to advance while she is waiting in the wings. She may sometimes resent the time she is spending away from her field.

"But I know that my family is more important than a few years on the career ladder," she consoles herself. This is the woman who may benefit from night courses at a local university or a job that she can do at home.

The Hope who chooses to work or who has to work for financial reasons may find herself saying, "I'm maintaining my career but missing out on my opportunities and duties as a mother." She misses the time she could be spending with her children and may envy the at-home mother. She may also find herself feeling very guilty, either from self-imposed guilt or guilt imposed by family members, friends, or "experts."

Employed Hope may need to cut down on activities other than family or job, making sure that her family is her primary ministry and priority.

3. Finally, the woman who answers yes to the first four questions and no to number five believes that women are equal and that there are no innate differences in the roles and responsibilities she and her husband must have. She may even prefer that the dad stay at home with the kids, like the father in the movie *Mr. Mom.*

Society is too few years away from traditional roles and has too few advocates of totally nontraditional roles for this woman to feel entirely comfortable with her choice. She will hear many voices from without, questioning her or making her feel guilty. Unless her husband is thoroughly in agreement with her beliefs, she will encounter conflicts there, too.

Whether a June Cleaver, a Hope Steadman, or a Mrs. Mr. Mom, the adolescence of women's roles leaves many of us as women in our own twilight zone, seeking to calm our own dissonance—to know what we should believe, to realize what we do believe, and to live in consonance with our conclusions. We must all answer the questions on our own and find the solutions that will help us to live in harmony with ourselves. ॐ

⇢⟫ Part VII ⟪⟵
Hush, Little Momma, Don't You Cry: God-Led Growth

Hush, little momma, don't you cry,
God'll make sure you grow by and by.

If your troubles seem without end,
You'll become a tree that bends in the wind.

If you let your Lord hold you so tight,
You'll draw your strength from God's holy might.

If you'll learn from the lessons God shows,
Wisdom and courage and strength will all grow.

If you remember the good gifts God gives,
You'll rest with the joy that in your heart lives. ⥱

➤➤ 25 ◄◄

As a Little Child

So Jesus called a child, had him stand in front of them, and said,
"I assure you that unless you change and become like children,
you will never enter the Kingdom of heaven."

—*Matthew 18:2-3 (GNB)*

➤➤ ◄◄

Tennis courts to a three-and-a-half-year-old are not large rectangles designated for a game using racquets and balls. Tennis courts to a three-and-a-half-year-old are for whatever comes to mind. And "throw-the-ball-through-the-hole-in-the-decrepit-net" was the game that came to Brian's mind.

I watched in quiet amusement as Brian tried to throw a tennis ball through a five-inch hole in the net. The problem was that he was standing several feet back from the net, so his success rate was pretty low. His frustration level, however, was quite high. I offered a small suggestion: "Put your hand close to the hole before you throw the ball." He put his right hand close to the hole, but tossed the ball with his left hand. Oh, well.

There's also the mother who told her small son to pick his cookie up off the floor before he stepped on it. And that's precisely what he did—picked his cookie up, put it down, and stepped on it.

Some of our favorite stories as parents are of the ways our children innocently misinterpret what we say. Not only do kids not have the experience with language that we do, but they are very literal-minded as well. I once explained to Daniel that Mimi wasn't home because she was getting her hair fixed. "Mimi's hair is broken?" he asked.

But more wonderful than the mind of a child is the heart of a child. I think this is what Jesus was referring to when he said, "Unless you change and become like children, you will never enter the Kingdom of heaven." It would not be delight I would be squealing with if someone tossed me into the air, yet a child is full of trust and unshackled by doubts. The child is not wondering as mom totes him around on her hip, *I'm not so sure I should be letting Mommy do this—what if she drops me?*

Forgiveness also comes much more easily to a child. She may be angry and crying at one moment, but happy and hugging the next.

Parents have cheap and easy access to a living book of modern-day parables as they live out their relationships with their children. This first struck me one evening, after a particularly trying day, as I stood holding and cuddling my toddler son. I recalled the events of the day: the pants flushed down the now-clogged toilet, the temper tantrum in the grocery store, the food on the floor, the fights over toys. But those were over now. They didn't matter. I was holding my child, soothing him and loving him. And then I glanced at a picture on the bedroom wall. There was Jesus, holding a lamb against his chest, soothing him and loving him.

How inadequate I felt at that moment. My reactions to the pressures of child-rearing are often far from Christlike. For that moment, I was the lamb. Jesus was holding me, soothing me, forgiving me—and as he did so, I felt his strength flowing into me, to help me with this awesome and precious responsibility of parenthood.

As I was strengthened, the parallel became real for me. My son had been a trial for me, in many ways, all the day—but, oh, how I still loved him! How many times do we, as God's children, cause disappointment and fall short of divine expectations? But, oh, how God still loves us!

I frequently now become aware of other ways in which my dealings with my children are like God's dealings with me. I think of God as I try to wash my children's hair. How much easier for them it would be if they would gently tilt their heads back as I rinse off the shampoo, but they stubbornly hold their heads down and cry at the injustice as water comes running down their faces. I think of God as I try to cleanse a child's scraped knee. I know I must clean it to keep infection away, but the child pulls away, kicking and screaming at my cruelty. How many times do we stubbornly refuse to do something, when God's way would be so much easier? How much of what happens to us would make perfect sense if we could see it through God's eyes? "For now we see through a glass, darkly; but then face to face: now I know in part; but then shall I know even as also I am known" (1 Corinthians 13:12, KJV).

Soon our children will be grown, and they will understand as we do now, more than they ever could as children. Someday we who are God's children will see more clearly and understand as we never could in our humanity. In the meantime, we can learn from our parent/child parables, realizing that God's wisdom is even further from our own than our children's wisdom is from ours—and our faith can grow accordingly. As we come before God on our knees, may we each truly come "as a little child." 🙢

⇒⟫ 26 ⟪⇐

From Daughter to Mother

I do not claim that I have already succeeded or have already become perfect. I keep striving to win the prize for which Christ Jesus has already won me to himself. Of course, my brothers, I really do not think that I have already won it; the one thing I do, however, is to forget what is behind me and do my best to reach what is ahead. So I run straight toward the goal in order to win the prize, which is God's call through Christ Jesus to the life above.
—Philippians 3:12–14 (GNB)

⇒⟫ ⟪⇐

As a society, Americans have few official "rites of passage." Jewish Americans still have bar mitzvahs and bat mitzvahs for their young men and women, but most of the rest of us have nothing official to pinpoint as our transition from childhood to adulthood. High school graduation roughly corresponds with transition into the voting age of eighteen, but that really is officially nothing more than a pat on the back for completing twelve years of school.

Yet as individuals, in the course of a lifetime, we go through numerous passages. Even once we reach adulthood, transitions are common and sometimes drastic: first job and subsequent career changes, marriage, death of family members or friends, moving from place to place, and parenthood.

Few of these transitions—good or bad—are we intellectually or emotionally prepared to cope with, but preparation can be a key to successfully maneuvering the course. I will be forever grateful for the open, enlightening, humorous, and wise premarital counseling that Lewwy and I received. We still have had to deal with the conflicts of marriage, but we knew what problems to expect and how to work through them.

Unfortunately, few couples receive preparenthood counseling. The passage into parenthood can seem like a passageway that is darker than we had expected: with darkness between the scattered windows, with lots of unexpected turns and dips, with no definitive maps yet many conflicting suggested routes, and sometimes very little company along the way. As I was making the transition, one of the deepest and most unexpected chasms I fell into was the twist in the passage from being the daughter of my mother to becoming a mother myself.

Two years after Lewwy and I married, my mother died. She and I had survived my teen years and had just begun to build a good adult relationship. My sister-in-law had joined the family and taught all of us to utter the words "I love you" frequently.

I grieved her loss and shed many tears, but I found comfort in the knowledge that she was spared the pain and worry involved in the postoperative treatment of cancer. I was immeasurably grateful that my relationship with her had ended on a good note and not on the cacophony of my thoughtless teen years.

Within a year, I became pregnant for the first time. I still thought of Mother at least once a day and still felt pain at her loss, but I was also wrapped up in excitement about my pregnancy. But because her death was still so recent, I blamed my bad dreams on a stage of grief and not on a stage of motherhood.

For more than a year after I became pregnant, I had bad dreams involving my mother and my children. The details of these dreams were much the same: my mother would come back and I would be happy to see her, and she to see me; but then the faults of my mother would loom up like ghosts, and I would be haunted by my mother and her imperfections. In many of these dreams, too, she would end up taking my children away with her up to heaven. Each time I would awaken from the dream, I was not only frightened by what had happened in the dream, but also grieved anew at the loss of my mother and hurt that my dreams of her were so negative.

It wasn't until later as I read of the adjustments that new mothers must make that I learned that all new mothers must once again cut the umbilical cord in order to create their own identity as a mother. We must separate ourselves from our mothers to become mothers ourselves.

What I feared, then, was that I had to copy my mother's example of mothering. I feared that I would simply be a repeat performance, and not a mother in my own right. I feared that I would make the same mistakes and that those mistakes would come between my children and me.

Well, several months after my boys were born, after being at their beck and call for all that time, my mind must have realized that yes, indeed, I was a mother in my own right—these little creatures were not going away, and I was the one they were looking up to to fulfill their every need.

Another step in that identity stage, though, I experienced with my mother-in-law and not my mother. My mother-in-law was wonderful about helping with the babies and cuddling them and quieting them and caring for them. But this insecure new mother didn't always want her to be so wonderful. I was jealous at times, fearful that she would be able to comfort them better than I could, afraid that they would want her more than they would want me.

Time again did wonders. Time and experience gave me the security I needed. Yes, Mimi is the one they can count on to give them Gummi Bears candies, to let them munch on popcorn as they watch as many videos as they'd like, and to give them attention and sweet talk when they need it, but that's what grandmas are for. I now know how important their relationship with her and with their Papa is—in addition to their relationship with me and my husband, not instead of it.

After four and a half years of motherhood, I have pretty much exited the transition period—although I do still marvel on occasion that when those three little kids are calling "Mommy," they mean me. More transitions are ahead, some expected, some unexpected. But as Paul says in Philippians, I'll keep running straight toward the goal, drawing upon God's strength to jump the hurdles as they come. ๛

→›› 27 ‹‹←
To My Hero

She is clothed with strength and dignity;
she can laugh at the days to come.
She speaks with wisdom,
and faithful instruction is on her tongue.
She watches over the affairs of her household
and does not eat the bread of idleness.
Her children arise and call her blessed;
her husband also, and he praises her:
"Many women do noble things,
but you surpass them all."
      —*Proverbs 31:25–29 (NIV)*
→›› ‹‹←

If I'm looking for a sentimental experience, I don't generally go to the Showbiz Pizza restaurant to see their life-size puppets provide musical entertainment. On this particular visit, however, the six-foot bear with her cheerleader outfit, pom-poms, and ponytails left me discreetly dabbing at my eyes as I sat surrounded by pizza-eating patrons. As this mechanical lead vocalist introduced her next selection as a tribute to all the mothers out there, all the unsung heroes of the world, I smiled and continued eating my pizza. However, when I tuned the bruin back in, she was singing, "You'll never know that you're my hero. . . ." As I listened to the song, I realized that no, my mother never will realize that she's my hero.

A mom can be a hero to a young child, an innocent child who still sees Mommy and Daddy through rose-colored glasses. Mommy can be the hero for fixing up boo-boos and making them all better, for taking the time to read and laugh with her little one, for knowing just how to fix a peanut butter and jelly sandwich, or for being warm and cuddly and soft.

But as a child reaches adolescence, those glasses often become muddied and "Motherrrr!" is anything but "cool" and "heroic." The teen years especially can be filled with conflict.

When son or daughter reaches young adulthood, dear old Mom may once again become a pretty neat person; but it's not until the daughter reaches a major milestone in her own life that Mom's nobility and heroism can once again reach superhuman proportions.

This major milestone is motherhood, when mother and daughter have something wondrous and challenging in common, when daughter-become-mother now understands those feelings her mother had, now smiles knowingly as she remembers the "curses" her mother often uttered in moments of frustration: "Just wait till you're a mother!" or, "I hope your children treat you like that—then you'll understand!"

Daughter can now appreciate those nights when mother sat up waiting for her to come home and why mother was both tearful and angry when daughter finally arrived. The daughter can now begin to understand the fears her mother had, the worries, the hopes, and the dreams. She can now see that many of her mother's "faults" were really just maternal attempts to protect and hold on to her offspring. She can relate to the pain and pride and joy that are part of the motherhood turf.

Never in the course of the shared lifetime is the potential greater for a rich mother-daughter relationship. And that's where my tears came from, for I never had the chance to share motherhood with my own mother.

My mother died less than a year before my first pregnancy. When I found out I was pregnant—and with twins at that—I was excited and proud, and wished that I could share the news with my mother. I was filled with questions about pregnancy and babies, about how her pregnancies and deliveries had gone, about what I had been like as a baby.

Since I was a "third child," my baby book was nonexistent. My father only knew of one picture of me under the age of twelve months, and that was a group shot of fifty Tobeys at a family reunion, with me in a stroller in the front row screaming at the top of my lungs. Was that what I was like as a baby? Probably. But with my mom gone—the one who remembered those little details—I felt like part of my own history was lost forever.

I imagined often during those days what it would have been like to have her close by. I knew how she would be anxious to help me, how she would be excited about being with Brian and Daniel. Perhaps most importantly, though, I imagined how my mother would mother me.

No one has ever made me feel as transparent as my mother. I knew during those days that she would take one look at me and see the stress that caring for two babies was putting on me. She would step in and help, not just to be nice, but because she cared about her own baby—me—and wanted to ease the strain. She would mother me, and I longed for the care and support that she would offer, to replenish the love I was giving to my babies.

My life with preschoolers became easier, and my longing changed from a longing for help to a longing to share my precious children with my mother. I wanted to show them off to her, to hear her bragging over their accomplishments and oohing and aahing over everything they did. I wanted to watch her laughing with them and teaching them her wonderful sense of humor. I wanted to see the pride in her eyes, to see the joy that I knew she would get from them, to see how much she would love them, and to know how much they would enjoy her.

I taught my toddlers to recognize my mother's picture and know who she was. I taught them to say "Oma," the German word for grandmother that my sister's children had used for my mother. The first time one of them said that very special name, I cried—at the joy of hearing him say her name, and at sadness that he would never know the special grandmother he could have had.

The longings are still there, and like the pain that is still there after six years, I know that they will never fully leave. Perhaps more longings and different pains lie in the future. Yet along with the pain is a new appreciation.

Proverbs 31 was a biblical passage my mother lived by, and the one that was chosen to be read at her funeral. My sister, my brother, and I do arise and call her blessed, but I have never before been as emphatic in saying that as I am now. She loved and served the Lord, and she taught her children to do so, too, by her words and by her deeds.

I'm a mother myself now. I finally understand the emotions that my mother felt for us, the worries, frustrations, and hopes that she had for all her children. And now, more than ever, I admire her.

Mother, I hope you do know that you are my hero. ❧

A Mother's "Exodus" or "Count Your Blessings"

The LORD *says,*
   "What accusation did your ancestors bring against me?
   What made them turn away from me?
They worshiped worthless idols
   and became worthless themselves.
They did not care about me,
   even though I rescued them from Egypt
   and led them through the wilderness:
   a land of deserts and sand pits,
   a dry and dangerous land
   where no one lives
   and no one will even travel.
I brought them into a fertile land,
   to enjoy its harvests and its other good things.
But instead they ruined my land;
   they defiled the country I had given them.
No other nation has ever changed its gods,
   even though they were not real.
But my people have exchanged me,
   the God who has brought them honor,
   for gods that can do nothing for them."
                                    —Jeremiah 2:5–7, 11 (GNB)

→≫ ≪←

Naive to the ways of the world on New Year's Eve, Lewwy and I joined up with his brother, Larry, and Larry's wife, Robin, for an evening of celebration. We had attempted that afternoon to get reservations at an appropriate restaurant, but half of the city of Richmond had already taken all the slots. That was fine, because we settled for a restaurant that didn't accept reservations—which is what the other half of the city of Richmond had done.

After an hour of standing in the cold, vacillating between restaurants and losing our place in line, hearing our stomachs growl, and feeling our knees weaken, we were no better off than we had been when we first parked the car. Lewwy and Larry, as always, were rolling with the punches and joking and laughing. Robin and I, on the other hand, though keeping our tempers basically in check, had plenty of words of grumble and complaint to make our feelings about the situation clear.

Clearing his throat for dramatic effect and attention, Larry said in his deepest and most serious tone, "I think now would be a good time for us to think of all the things we're thankful for." His sentiment was wonderful, but I had no appreciation for it.

Certainly he was right. Counting our blessings could have put things into perspective. But in the midst of my frustration, I didn't feel like stopping and counting my blessings. I even felt like wallowing a bit: I deserve to be angry and don't anyone try to stop me!

I daresay that is how the Israelites felt as they wandered in the wilderness: we deserve to be angry and don't anyone try to stop us!

I used to be quite judgmental when I read the book of Exodus: "You crazy Israelites! How can you be questioning God? Why, just fifteen chapters ago God produced water for you from a rock. Just eighteen chapters ago God miraculously opened the waters of the Red Sea for you alone! There were plagues on the Egyptians and deliverance from those brutal taskmasters, and here you are griping! God made good water from bitter water, and sent you manna and quails, and you are building a gold bull because Moses is taking too long on Mount Sinai! What ingrates you are!"

Then I began wondering what "The Exodus of Mary Tobey Marsh" would look like. Time speeds by from chapter to chapter as I read the biblical book of Exodus, but for the Israelites time crept slowly and wearily by as they wandered without a permanent home. Would a book of my life look like theirs?

The Exodus of Mary Tobey Marsh

Chapter 1: God cleanses her from all sin and she gratefully accepts Jesus Christ as her Savior and Lord. She grows in her Christian walk.

Chapter 2: She willingly gets trapped in a relationship that does not bring honor to God.

Chapter 3: God allows the relationship to end and teaches her that singleness is good. God later leads her to a wonderful, God-loving husband.

Chapter 4: She often gets tired of marriage and the work it involves and is willing to settle for mediocrity.

Chapter 5: God keeps her plugging along and growing, in her marriage and in her Christian walk.

Chapter 6: She adopts a materialistic philosophy: No, money doesn't bring happiness, but neither does lack of money. She wishes for more money.

Chapter 7: She prays for children; God grants her pregnancy, and leads her safely through early hemorrhaging and her pregnancy to the birth of healthy twin baby boys.

Chapter 8: She grumbles at the work and stress and difficulty in caring for two babies.

And then there are the hourly sagas:

8:00 a.m. God blesses her with wisdom about patience as she has her daily devotional.

8:30 a.m. She complains about the car that pulled out in front of her and made her miss the stoplight.

9:00 a.m. God provides unexpected money for the household bills.

9:30 a.m. She is envious of her friend's new car.

The Israelites in the wilderness have nothing on the life of Mary Tobey Marsh. No, I did not fashion a gold bull as an idol, but I do have a house that I long to have wonderfully decorated. As soon as the next chapter begins, I forget the way God blessed me in the earlier chapters.

Preschool motherhood can be a time of wilderness chapters: strong emotions, difficult trials, ever-present fatigue, and crazy hormones. In the midst of the frustrations, when the baby has awakened for the fifth time that night, when the toddler has used mommy's make-up for his latest wall mural, or when a husband asks, "What do you do all day anyway?"—it is not easy for a mother to count her blessings. It's tough to want to do anything but cry or scream or run out of the house nevermore to return.

Nowhere is our need to count our blessings stated more succinctly and beautifully than in the old gospel hymn "Count Your Blessings":

When upon life's billows you are tempest tossed,
When you are discouraged, thinking all is lost,
Count your many blessings, name them one by one,
And it will surprise you what the Lord hath done.

Are you ever burdened with a load of care?
Does the cross seem heavy you are called to bear?
Count your many blessings, ev'ry doubt will fly,
And you will be singing as the days go by.

When you look at others with their lands and gold,
Think that Christ has promised you His wealth untold;
Count your many blessings, money cannot buy
Your reward in heaven, nor your home on high.

So, amid the conflict, whether great or small,
Do not be discouraged, God is over all;
Count your many blessings, angels will attend,
Help and comfort give you to your journey's end.

Count your blessings, name them one by one:
Count your blessings, see what God hath done;
Count your blessings, name them one by one;
Count your many blessings, see what God hath done.[28]

I must admit, however, that I often resent it when someone says to me in the midst of a crisis, "Could be worse!" or "Look on the bright side" or even "Count your blessings!" Even though I know they're right, that's not what I want to hear in the heat of the moment. Fortunately, though, because I know how true the count-your-blessings concept is, the Lord is making it a part of my habitual reaction: I will sometimes think to myself as I sigh, "I suppose I do have a lot to be thankful for." (But don't anybody else say that to me!)

Perhaps one of our best offensive weapons in the fight against human self-pity and discouragement is preparation: if we can count our blessings frequently in our more lucid moments, then we can make the thoughts of our blessings more a part of us, more natural, and ever-present in our subconscious. We can enumerate our blessings, big or small, so they will be in the front of our minds when the trials start pouring in.

And as we count our blessings, we mustn't forget to count our "well-disguised blessings": our trials. As James explains, "My

104

brothers, consider yourselves fortunate when all kinds of trials come your way, for you know that when your faith succeeds in facing such trials, the result is the ability to endure. Make sure that your endurance carries you all the way without failing, so that you may be perfect and complete, lacking nothing" (James 1:2–4, GNB). James also points out, "Happy is the person who remains faithful under trials, because when he succeeds in passing such a test, he will receive as his reward the life which God has promised to those who love him" (James 1:12, GNB).

Although my blessings and trials are frequently one and the same—named Daniel, Brian, and Rachel—I know God can help me focus on the blessedness of motherhood rather than the trials. Let it not be said of me what the psalmist said of the Israelites:

> We have sinned as our ancestors did;
> we have been wicked and evil.
> Our ancestors in Egypt did not understand God's wonderful acts;
> they forgot the many times he showed them his love,
> and they rebelled against the Almighty at the Red Sea.
> But he saved them, as he had promised,
> in order to show his great power.
> He gave a command to the Red Sea,
> and it dried up;
> he led his people across on dry land.
> He saved them from those who hated them;
> he rescued them from their enemies.
> But the water drowned their enemies;
> not one of them was left.
> Then his people believed his promises
> and sang praises to him.
> But they quickly forgot what he had done
> and acted without waiting for his advice.
> —*Psalm 106:6–13 (GNB)*

May your Exodus differ drastically from the Exodus of the Israelites. ह≫

⇥≫ Notes ≪⇤

1 C. S. Lewis, *Surprised by Joy* (New York: Harcourt, Brace & World, Inc., 1955), p. 131.

2 L. M. Montgomery, *Anne of Green Gables* (New York: Bantam Books; L. C. Page & Company, Inc., 1908).

3 Paul C. Nagel, *The Adams Women: Abigail and Louisa Adams, Their Sisters and Daughters* (New York: Oxford University Press, 1987), p. 265.

4 *Ibid.,* p. 266.

5 *Ibid.,* p. 267.

6 *Ibid.,* pp. 270–72.

7 Blayne Cutler, "Rock-A-Buy Baby," *American Demographics* (January 1990), p. 37.

8 Nagel, *The Adams Women,* pp. 54–55.

9 Madeleine L'Engle, *Two-Part Invention: The Story of a Marriage* (New York: Farrar, Straus & Giroux, 1988), p. 155.

10 Two helpful Christian household management books: Emilie Barnes, *Survival for Busy Women: Establishing Efficient Home Management* (Eugene, Oregon: Harvest House Publishers, 1986); and Sandra Felton, *The Messies Manual: The Procrastinator's Guide to Good Housekeeping* (Old Tappan, New Jersey: Fleming H. Revell Company, 1984).

11 Verses 1–3 are from *Tomie dePaola's Mother Goose* (New York: G. P. Putnam's Sons, 1985), p. 30. Verses 4–5 are by the author.

12 Dr. James C. Dobson, *Parenting Isn't for Cowards: Dealing Confidently with the Frustrations of Child-Rearing* (Waco, Texas: Word Books Publisher, 1987), p. 184.

13 *Ibid.,* pp. 186–187.

14 Charles R. Swindoll, *You and Your Child* (Nashville: Thomas Nelson Publishers, 1977), p. 20.

15 *Ibid.,* p. 24.

16 *Ibid.*

17 Tomie dePaola's *Mother Goose,* pp. 102–103.

18 *American Heritage Dictionary,* New College Edition, s.v. "vocation."

19 *Ibid.*

20 Stanley C. Baldwin, *Take This Job and Love It* (Downers Grove, Illinois: InterVarsity Press, 1988), pp. 89–97.

21 *Ibid.,* pp. 109–119.

22 *Ibid.,* pp. 111–113.

23 *Ibid.,* p. 111.

24 *Ibid.,* pp. 111–112.

25 *Ibid.,* p. 112.

26 *Ibid.*

27 *Ibid.,* pp. 112–113.

28 "Count Your Blessings," words by Johnson Oatman, Jr., 1897. This hymn is found in a number of hymnals including *Baptist Hymnal* (Nashville: Convention Press, 1975).

⇒» Bibliography «⇐

Baldwin, Stanley C. *Take This Job & Love It.* Downers Grove, Illinois: InterVarsity Press, 1988.

Barnes, Emilie. *Survival for Busy Women: Establishing Efficient Home Management.* Eugene, Oregon: Harvest House Publishers, 1986.

Campbell, Ross. *How to Really Love Your Child.* Wheaton, Illinois: Victor Books, 1977.

Cutler, Blayne. "Rock-A-Buy Baby." *American Demographics,* January 1990, pp. 36–39.

Dobson, James. *Dare to Discipline.* Wheaton, Illinois: Tyndale House Publishers, 1973.

Dobson, James. *Hide or Seek: How to Build Self-Esteem in Your Child.* Old Tappan, New Jersey: Fleming H. Revell Company, 1979.

Dobson, James C. *Parenting Isn't for Cowards: Dealing Confidently with the Frustrations of Child-Rearing.* Waco, Texas: Word Books Publisher, 1987.

Felton, Sandra. *The Messies Manual: The Procrastinator's Guide to Good Housekeeping.* Old Tappan, New Jersey: Fleming H. Revell Company, 1983.

Keirsey, David, and Marilyn Bates. *Please Understand Me: Character and Temperament Types.* Del Mar, California: Prometheus Nemesis Book Company, 1984.

Kimmel, Tim. *Legacy of Love: A Wake-Up Call.* Portland, Oregon: Multnomah Press, 1989.

Leman, Kevin. *Making Children Mind Without Losing Yours.* Old Tappan, New Jersey: Fleming H. Revell, 1983.

Leman, Kevin. *Bonkers: Why Women Get Stressed Out and What They Can Do About It.* New York: Dell Publishing Co., 1989.

L'Engle, Madeleine. *Two-Part Invention: The Story of a Marriage.* New York: Farrar, Straus & Giroux, 1988.

Lewis, C. S. *Surprised by Joy: The Shape of My Early Life.* New York: Harcourt, Brace, Jovanovich, 1956.

Montgomery, Lucy Maud. *Anne of Green Gables.* New York: Bantam Books; L. C. Page & Company, Inc., 1976.

Nagel, Paul C. *The Adams Women: Abigail & Louisa Adams, Their Sisters and Daughters.* New York: Oxford University Press, 1987.

Neff, LaVonne. *One of a Kind: Making the Most of Your Child's Uniqueness.* Portland, Oregon: Multnomah Press, 1988.

Swindoll, Charles R. *You and Your Child.* 2nd ed. Nashville, Tennessee: Thomas Nelson Publishers, 1982.